SURVIVING THE RAGING FIRE

Keeping Our Faith
in a Time of Spiritual Decline

PAT SCOTT

To Kathryn, Blessings, Pat Scott

Published By

21ST CENTURY CHRISTIAN

2809 Granny White Pike
Nashville, TN 37204

SURVIVING THE RAGING FIRE

Published by 21st Century Christian, 2809 Granny White Pike, Nashville, TN 37204.

ISBN 0-89098-182-5

To Scott and Grant Tucker,
my precious grandsons, whose young lives are in
the process of being molded.
We pray continually that you will grow to be
strong and faithful Christian men.

Contents

Acknowledgements

My gratitude goes to Flossye Gagneux, my ever-faithful reader, and to Dr. Don Umphrey, professor of English at Southern Methodist University, for his expertise and counsel. Incalculable credit goes to Carol Pauley for her ongoing assistance in so many areas of my writing.

Preface

The Old Testament described men and women who were supposed to be God's people, but they voluntarily joined the pagan community. Their lack of commitment to God separated them from Him. Because of that separation, they no longer had the benefit of His power, and they were swallowed up by those pagan cultures.

By contrast, the New Testament told of a time when Christians were persecuted for their commitment to their faith. Those people remained steadfast, even though they were scattered. Their adversity caused their faith to thrive, attract others and spread everywhere.

Recent studies have indicated that a large percentage of people claiming to be Christians today exhibit values that are no longer distinctive from those of the general populace of pagans. They reflect approximately as many divorces, abortions, and addictions. Those statistics speak loudly of a lack of commitment to our beliefs. It has taken this country only slightly more than two hundred years to forget its heritage of religious principles.

It is urgent that God's people begin to ask themselves whether they may be contributing to the moral and spiritual decline in this country. We must find a way to strengthen our resolve to live what we say that we believe. If our lives do not reflect our Christianity, we will be integrated into a decadent society and be separated from our God—and our hope.

God's people can expect to survive and thrive, regardless of the culture around us—if we keep our perspective about our purpose for being here. God has the power to control the raging fire of infidelity sweeping our land, but if His people willingly plunge into the flames, no one will be left to save. God will not force us to be faithful, but He will empower us if we are willing.

WHEN THE WAYS OF THE WORLD
SEEM TO BE WINNING

"Don't be afraid, those who are with us are more than those who are with them."
II Kings 6:16

The mountains of northern New Mexico, thick with Ponderosa and Blue Spruce trees, refresh and invigorate vacationers with cool clean air. Eagerly, I opened the car windows to enjoy the crisp breeze while winding through narrow mountain roads that approach my cabin. Upon arrival, I eagerly began unloading the car. Suddenly, the serenity was interrupted by the obtrusive sound of the telephone. It was a neighbor who lived on another mountain about two miles away. "Pat, don't you know that there is a raging forest fire just up the mountain from your place?" Indeed, I had not known!

A forest fire can start from only a small spark and slowly smolder for a while before bursting into a fierce and dangerous fire. Often such fires are ignited when lightning strikes a tree. Whatever the initial cause, the dry stubble and underbrush are very combustible sources to fuel the fire. They embrace the flame and race enthusiastically with it among the tall green trees.

After receiving the warning from my neighbor, I dashed back outside to verify his unbelievable message. Within minutes a special unit of firefighters, called "hot shots," came marching down my road. They were wearing their big boots and special jackets, and they were carrying axes to cut a firebreak. A firebreak is a wide swath made by cutting away trees and underbrush. Denied its fuel, a fire can sometimes be contained. One of the firefighters announced that he would be staying with me just in case evacuation became necessary. Periodically, he would talk on his walkie-talkie radio to the other firefighters who had gone further up the mountain.

A forest fire cannot be taken lightly. Not only can it move rapidly, it can cut off the escape route. It threatens everything in its path. The pristine beauty of the area becomes blackened with thick rolling smoke, and darkness resembling night invades the land. The roaring flames of the raging fire swiftly swallow homes. Many animals die, and human life is sometimes lost as well. So, the firefighter turned to me and said, "Prepare to evacuate!"

Vehicles began chugging up the road leading to my house. The fireman looked dismayed. Curiosity seems to be a common thread that runs through humanity. Like moths drawn to a light, neighbors were swarming to see how serious the blaze would be.

I stood in disbelief. How could there be such a serious fire so close by when I had not even smelled the smoke? I had not felt the heat. Perhaps I was so accustomed to the summer temperatures in Dallas that heat was not noticeable. Possibly, I had been enjoying the comfortable mountain surroundings so much that I was lulled into complacency!

Sometimes, Christians find themselves enjoying this life so much that they close their eyes to Satan's raging fire of sin and immorality even as it roars around them. The stubble and underbrush of the world have embraced the flames and now run with enthusiasm, threatening to overpower God's people. The billowing darkness settles over the land, obscuring our vision. Living day after day in such close proximity to the conditions surrounding Satan's raging fire of sin tends to deaden our senses to the heat. Gradually, we may begin to look similar to those darkened, damaged trees that have already been consumed by the fire, even though we hadn't even felt the heat.

Like a forest fire, this raging fire of sin and worldliness threatens everything in its path. It is destroying homes, families, and children as they succumb and are ravenously swallowed up by its overpowering flames.

The dry stubble and the underbrush of the world fuel Satan's fires. Since they are already dead, they are not sensitive to the cruel deeds and injustices spewed by the flames. They don't weigh their actions by any standard of right or wrong. They lap up the ways of Satan and rush on toward their next pleasure, destroying anything or anyone in their paths. They see no reason to hesitate as they encourage all their fellow stubble to ignite and spread their message of sin and destruction.

Such fires were burning furiously in the days of Noah in the Old Testament. Everyone except Noah was doing whatever it took to ensure happiness for themselves. Genesis 6:5 said, *"The Lord saw how great man's wickedness on the earth had become, and that every inclination of the thoughts of his heart was only evil all the time."* It is surprising and frightening to observe how few people in Noah's time were able to remain unburned during that time of raging fire. Genesis 6:7 said, *"Noah was a righteous man, blameless among the people of his time, and he walked with God."* This passage would indicate that Noah had no friend to encourage or support him in his righteous ways. It seems as if the raging fire had somehow missed one lonely tree and left it to stand tall and green against black-ened stumps and stubs. Life for Noah must have been a very solitary journey in such a situation, even with his sons and wife. It couldn't have been easy for Noah to hold a conviction that conflicted with the world around him.

MENTAL IMAGES ARE STORED

It is impossible to survive such a fire without getting at least a few smudges. The environment created by the rag-ing fire affects us more than most of us would like to believe. Our minds absorb the images and words, storing them as would the memory chip in a computer. Did you ever hear a musical jingle and have it haunt you all day long? Advertisers know the power of the images and words that they show us. That is exactly why billions of dollars are spent for advertising. Yet, when media moguls are rebuked for showing violence, bad language, and immorality, they protest by saying that people are not affected by merely seeing such things.

> *Our minds absorb the images and words, storing them, as would the memory chip in a computer.*

Things that we see repeatedly become commonplace to us. Even horribly sinful conduct, when seen frequently enough, will dull our conscience to sin. Sin can begin to seem acceptable—perhaps even desirable! When one word of profanity was used in "Gone With the Wind" many years ago, there was shock across the land. But today movies are filled with profanity, and producers think that films will not be successful without such language. We don't hear many voices of protest. The national conscience has been dulled, and we will store those words and images.

In Exodus 32:4-6, we read:

Aaron took what they handed him and made it into an idol cast in the shape of a calf, fashioning it with a tool. Then they said, "These are your gods, O Israel, who brought you up out of Egypt." When Aaron saw this, he built an altar in front of the calf and announced, "Tomorrow there will be a festival to the Lord." So the next day the people rose early and sacrificed burnt offerings and presented fellowship offerings. Afterward they sat down to eat and drink and got up to indulge in revelry.

Where do you suppose those Hebrew people got the idea that a golden image of a calf could make a difference in their lives? Certainly they did not get that idea from their God, for He had forbidden such conduct. Indeed, they had lived for many years among the idols of the Egyptians. Idols had become commonplace to them.

> *Where do you suppose those Hebrew people got the idea that a golden image of a calf could make a difference in their lives?*

In Memphis, the ancient capital city of Egypt, there has now been excavated a great temple built to the sacred bull Apis. The Egyptians worshipped a bull. Underneath the temple was found an avenue eleven hundred and twenty feet long. On each side of the avenue were sixty-four burial chambers—no, not for Pharaohs. In the center of each burial chamber was either a red or black granite sarcophagus, and inside each sarcophagus was a sacred bull.

Are we ever free from the influences that have stamped themselves indelibly into our memories?

The pomp and splendor of the worship of Apis was an impressive sight to behold. The Israelites had seen the Egyptian people, even those who held great power, worshipping the bull. Of course, God had always taught them that they were to have no other gods. The teachings of God were clear, but man has always had an incredible penchant for rationalizing away the clear commandments of God.

And so there were the people of God at Sinai, free at last from the demands and the influence of the Egyptians—or were they? Are we ever free from the influences that have stamped themselves indelibly into our memories? Their minds had been given the poison of idolatry. Therefore, when Moses seemed to have vanished upon the mountain, they fell back upon what was familiar to them—the wicked worship of the bull of Egypt.

Even those who are supposed to be God's people can do unthinkable and wicked things. They are not at all beyond being influenced by the dark deeds of the world around them. They need a firebreak to give them safe distance from the dangers of wickedness. God's people are at risk when they become too comfortable with the ways of the world.

When there is a raging fire of immorality sweeping the land, God's people have to be keenly aware of the threat. With any fire there is likelihood that it will spread. It may gain so much momentum that it might even jump the fire-break and invade the unburned trees. One of the greatest threats to God's people today is not the danger without, but the danger within. The sparks from the fires of Satan are smoldering on our side of the firebreak.

The George Barna survey recently asked one hundred and fifty-two questions of two very separate groups. The first group was made up of people who considered them-selves religious and attended church regularly. The sec-ond group did not consider themselves religious and almost never attended church. His findings were shock-ing and disappointing. He found that there were no more divorces among those who never attended church than among those who faithfully attended church. He found that there were equally as many abortions in each group. He found only one percentage point difference in the number of those who gambled.

Even without the Barna survey, it is noticeable over on the green side of the firebreak that we don't mind hand-ing over five or more dollars to be entertained by immoral behavior and language that we wouldn't think of using—at least not yet! We say, "Oh, it's only artistic expression." Or we say, "It was a good movie; you just have to overlook the language, nudity and sex scenes." We even find ourselves recommending it to our friends.

It is also disturbing that many parents take young children with them to see entertainment that is totally unsuitable. In a recent letter written to the editor of a newspaper, the writer was distressed because he had been to an R-rated movie and had seen parents who had brought their four-year old child. He was horrified that the parents had no better judgment than to allow their child to see such excessive violence and bad language. This generation may be sacrificing the souls of its precious children upon the altar of television, movies, and the Internet.

There is a passage in Psalm 11:3 in which the writer asked, *"When the foundations are being destroyed, what can the righteous do?"* One thing that the righteous can do is to be who they say they are! Our foundations are eroding because the raging fire is affecting God's people more than they are affecting it. It has been said, "We must live what we believe or we will soon believe what we live."

Recently, a mother who views herself as Christian and wants her family to be faithful said that her child had been in trouble at school (a private Christian school) for using a bad word. The teacher couldn't imagine where the child

> *"When the foundations are being destroyed, what can the righteous do?"*
> —*Psalm 11:3*

had heard that word. The mother, with no apologetic tone in her voice, said that it was a word that she and her husband sometimes used. One would wonder why she would spend so much money to send her child to an expensive private Christian school and then expose her to profanity at home. The child will eventually not know what to believe.

God's people must live what they believe, or there will be no firebreak—and no reason for one!

OUR CHANGING WORLD

Many in our society have embraced the raging fire of immorality and spiritual decline and are spreading it throughout the land. It is painful to watch our nation move away from being a Christian nation. We seem to watch helplessly as foreign religions move in and actually grow. Such religions with their gods will naturally have equal protection under the constitution and, frequently, protection for them will automatically be one of the reasons that Christianity is pushed out of public institutions. In our tolerant society, Christians sound prejudiced if they dare object. As a result, we are witnessing the paradox of watching Russia's school system eager to have Bibles in their classrooms, while the Holy Scriptures are off limits in the public schools of the United States.

> *God's people must live what they believe, or there will be no fire- break—and no reason for one!*

The residual effects of Satan's raging fire translate into heartbreaking injustices across our land. The most painful injustice that we helplessly watch is the increase in abuse of little children. The newspapers almost daily tell stories of the deaths of very young children, fresh from God, who have been abused, tortured, and killed.

Also, homosexuality has been given credence by the media as being an accept-able lifestyle. Some judges are deciding that homosex-uals should be given access to our children in public schools and perhaps the Boy Scout programs. When

> "Why do you make me look at injustice? Why do you tolerate wrong?"
> —Habakkuk 1:3

God says that a certain conduct is "detestable" to Him, He has not been known to change His mind just because time has elapsed.

Abortion, even late term abortion, has been deemed an acceptable practice. Human life is gradually being deval-ued. Newspapers have all carried the story of the young woman who gave birth to a baby, killed it, threw it into the trash and returned to the dance. She was sentenced to two years in jail. By contrast, in another court, a man who had tortured and killed animals was sentenced to serve twelve years in prison.

When God is not valued, human life is devalued. When we feel overwhelmed with so many injustices in our world, we, like Habakkuk, want to ask God, "Why do you make me look at injustice? Why do you tolerate wrong?" (Habakkuk 1:3). We wonder whether God will allow this nation to go the way that so many nations have gone to destruction. And what about those of us who are His people? Perhaps like Abraham, we may ask, "For the sake of fifty righteous souls would you spare the country?" What can we expect from God in times like these?

We would like to think that God would in some way smite the evil forces of Satan that are ravaging our land. Many people are diligently trying to turn back the forces of Satan. Many of us pray fervently that God will help us win this battle.

Our battle is not only for our own souls, but also for the souls of our children and grandchildren. Perhaps circumstances such as these are what the apostle Paul meant when he spoke in Ephesians 6:12: "*For our struggle is not against flesh and blood, but against the rulers, against the authorities, and against the powers of this dark world and against the spiritual forces of evil in the heavenly realms.*" When the ways of the world seem to be winning, we tend to focus on the public figures who seem to be fanning the flames. We see them as our enemies when in reality it is Satan. The Hollywood celebrities, athletes, etc., are merely the stubble and underbrush fueling Satan's ambitions to ambush the faithful.

COME OUT AND BE SEPARATE

This is a time when God's people need to be aware that the wind is blowing sparks among us to smolder, causing spotty fires. Recently, one firefighter in California lamented that it was so difficult to control the fires there, because there were so many small fires rather than just one large fire. Among God's people those smoldering sparks are sometimes allowed to burst into flame, and eventually there may be many small brush fires.

Christians have been called out of the world to be a holy people. We should never act like dry stubble and underbrush that fuel Satan's fire. To be holy means "to be set apart to God" while still living among those who may choose to love worldliness. Even among our close acquaintances, many are on the verge of becoming dry stubble, and they are vulnerable to the flying sparks. Not only must we live among the flying sparks, we must live close enough to the dry stubble and underbrush to love their souls—which means that we cannot become monks and isolate ourselves in some remote region. Our task can become quite a balancing act.

The contrast between a Christian and the world often causes the world to feel uncomfortable. That contrast is likely to cause the world to take one of two actions. They will first try to assimilate us back into the world—either by ridicule or subtle persuasion. If that fails, they will try to destroy us. Today, Christians are being labeled as extremists or the religious "right." Either label lumps us all into the same category as people who are not considered reasonable or sophisticated like "normal" people.

Without a doubt, the world will not like God's people. Jesus put it this way in John 15:19: *"If you belonged to the world, it would love you as its own. As it is, you do not belong to the world, but I have chosen you out of the world. That is why the world hates you."* Obviously, the world has never liked God's people.

In I Peter 4:4, Peter wrote to Christians who were being persecuted, explaining to them how they were viewed by the world. It is as fitting today as it was then. *"They think it strange that you do not plunge with them into the same flood of dissipation, and they heap abuse upon you."* Peter's message would sound appropriate in churches across America. He was describing ungodly people who had no knowledge of God or respect for His authority. In II Peter 2:12, he said, *"But these men blaspheme in matters they do not understand. They are like brute beasts, creatures of instinct, born only to be caught and destroyed, and like beasts, they too will perish."*

The people whose lives are played out in the media are often those who live, not by moral standards, but by human instinct. They think that if it feels good, it must be right. Their "god" would want them to be happy, and they want nothing to do with any other God. For them the word "authority" has gone out of style.

> *God never intended that His people "blend in."*

We are not the first Christians to live in such a world, but still we ask, "What can we expect of God in times like these?" We can learn from the biblical examples of God's relationship with His people.

The Israelites of the Old Testament were sometimes not rescued by God because they willingly assimilated themselves into the pagan culture. Their disobedience caused God to allow temporary victory by their enemies. A "temporary victory" might be approximately seventy years—a fact that should not give us great comfort.

The Israelites frequently attempted to embrace both the God of Abraham and the gods of the pagan world. That compromise is one that can be very tempting to Christians today. From the earliest times, God forbade that arrangement. God never intended that His people "blend in." In fact, He meant for them to look different from the world.

Christians do not use saws and axes to cut a firebreak between themselves and the world. It is the way that we live our lives that will separate us from the

> *It is the way we live our lives that will separate us from the raging fire.*

raging fire. If we live like the world, there will be no contrast and no holiness to distinguish us from the worldly stubble and underbrush. There will be no firebreak.

The Lord will not be pleased if we join the dry brush and stubble carrying the fire of immorality and spiritual decline. In I Peter 2:11, Peter spoke to those hurting Christians saying, "*I urge you as aliens and strangers in the world to abstain from sinful desires which war against your soul.*" Obviously, the world will entice us, and we will have "sinful desires" to assimilate ourselves into their ranks.

The raging fire reaches for us and tries to make us a part of its destructive forces. As we live in these times, the world will try to win us back or destroy us. Paul wrote to the church at Corinth in II Corinthians 11: 3, *"But I am afraid that just as Eve was deceived by the serpent's cunning, your minds may somehow be led astray from your sincere and pure devotion to Christ."*

Satan knows just which flavor of temptation to wave before us. Your flavor may not be the same as mine. When we think that we cannot be snared, that is exactly when we are most vulnerable. In I Corinthians 10:12, Paul also wrote, *"If you think you are standing firm, be careful that you don't fall!"* Tranquilized by a rather comfortable life, we don't seem to feel the danger of Satan's raging fire—his cunning ability to influence our reasoning and our actions.

In the Garden of Gethsemane, while Jesus was praying fervently and suffering great anguish, his closest followers were sleeping. You would think that they would also have been praying and feeling deep concern. Sleeping at such a critical time! It is incomprehensible!

Yet here we are, living in a time when our allegiance to the Lord is being tested daily through a myriad of offerings. Are we praying, or are we sleeping? Through the example of the sleeping disciples at Gethsemane, Jesus may be saying to us, *"Watch and pray so that you will not fall into temptation. The spirit is willing, but the body is weak"* (Matthew 26:41).

The firebreak will be maintained only if we live what we say we believe.

SAPPED, SINGED, AND SEARED

If you do not stand firm in your faith,
you will not stand at all.

Isaiah 7:9

To narrowly escape a blazing inferno would not only be an unforgettable experience, it would likely teach a few lasting lessons. Lise Bohannon, a young waitress, was one of the few who escaped a fire at the Beverly Hills Supper Club in Southgate, Kentucky in May 1977. A structure that sprawled like a maze housed the restaurant, which boasted a number of separate dining rooms. While refilling a customer's coffee cup, she overheard one of the men at the table say, "There seems to be a fire in one of the other dining rooms. Perhaps we should leave." His voice sounded so calm and unconcerned that her first impulse was to continue her work. After all, she didn't want to be viewed as an alarmist. To over-react would make her look foolish. Then, she changed her mind. She decided to get her purse and just step outside for a few minutes as a precaution.

In order to exit the building one had to go out a single doorway and then walk down a stairway, through a small foyer and out the front door. As Lise Bohannon started toward the stairway, she realized that about thirty people were already ahead of her! Perhaps there had been reason for alarm! As she merged with the departing customers on the stairs, she glanced back. To her horror she saw a mass of humanity pushing and shoving in a desperate attempt to reach the stairway.

She could hardly believe that the situation could have escalated so quickly. As she walked out into the cool night air, she turned to look back at where she had just been so routinely serving customers. Flames could be seen darting behind closed windows, and thick black smoke filled the building.

Many of the people trying to leave the building were overcome by smoke. Others were likely trampled in the frantic exodus. The rapid spread of that fire killed one hundred and sixty-four people who had intended to enjoy an evening of delightful dining.

That tragedy forever changed Lise Bohannon. No one will ever need to coerce her to be cautious about the danger of fire. She now has conviction about the danger of fire! She firmly believes that one could easily be trapped by a fast-moving inferno, and she is acting on that conviction. Lise has adopted a number of precautions in order to feel more secure. Her advice has implications for us as we contemplate another type of fire—the fire of moral and spiritual decline.

REAL CONVICTION IS FLAME RESISTANT

When we are genuinely convicted about something, it will change us. We will do things differently. If it doesn't change us, we are not really convicted. And if it doesn't change us, there is no reason to be convicted!

> When we are genuinely convicted about something, it will change us.

When Jesus spoke with the rich ruler in Luke 18:18-30, He recognized that the man lacked genuine conviction. The ruler was convicted enough to want the prize but not enough to act on his conviction.

It is not unusual for man to treasure certain earthly goods or desires more than he loves Jesus. Like the ruler, there are many things that we will sacrifice, but we prefer to decide what that sacrifice will be. But Jesus said to the rich ruler, "You still lack one thing." Jesus wasn't interested in the man's possessions but in the man's heart. Our conviction may not be genuine enough to keep us faithful in a time of spiritual decline—especially if there are things that we treasure more than Jesus.

Unlike the rich ruler, the apostle Paul held a deep conviction about Jesus. He fervently believed that the struggles of this life would eventually be supplanted by a glorious heavenly reward. Paul not only spoke about his conviction, he allowed his conviction to change his life completely.

Paul had a promising career, and he had done much study to prepare himself for that career. He was a Pharisee and would no doubt have been an important leader, but he left it all. We may feel rather uncomfortable when we contemplate a level of conviction and commitment that would cause us to make such a change.

Paul had influence and prestige among the Pharisees. No doubt, he had friends and family who would consider him an outcast because of his changed life. For a time, Paul was almost friendless, because the Christians feared him. Can we imagine losing family and friends because of our conviction?

Losing a career, family, and friends would be very painful, but to endure scorn, beatings, and prison would really be a test of fire. Most of us shudder at the thought of enduring such a test of our conviction. Yet, it is helpful to know that people such as Paul did remain true to their conviction—no matter what the consequences.

We need to read about such faithful Christians repeatedly in order to strengthen our own conviction. And we need to read the promises of God again and again, lest we become dry stubble, susceptible to the flames of moral and spiritual decline. Jesus responded to the waning conviction of the rich ruler by saying, *"No one who has left home or wife or brothers or parents or children for the sake of the kingdom of God will fail to receive many times as much in this age, and in the age to come, eternal life"* (Luke 18:30). That promise made by Jesus would suggest that even in this life on earth we could expect a better life if we live for our King.

Human logic would never have conceived the divine truth of Jesus' promise that a sacrificial life is better than a selfish one. But every Christian martyr that we meet in the New Testament is an example of that truth. Stephen was filled with hope even as he was being stoned; and the apostles were never deterred by their floggings. God obviously infuses a strength and joy into those who

> *Human logic would never have conceived the divine truth of Jesus' promise that a sacrificial life is better than a selfish one.*

refuse to have their conviction colored by the opinions of the world.

SAPPING OUR VITALITY AND CONVICTION

Lise Bohannon survived that restaurant fire in Kentucky, and she is convicted about the danger of fire. She has taken specific steps to be better prepared for any future fire. She now points out the foolishness of assuming that fire won't spread. She urges us to be aware of our surroundings and to know how to find the exit. She isn't recommending paranoia, but vigilance. She said that when she travels, she now carries a small flashlight to help find an exit when she is in unfamiliar surroundings. Her third piece of advice was "Don't ignore danger. Respond quickly!"

Her warnings should get our attention as we watch a threatening fire. As Christians, we may assume that a few smoldering sparks on our side of the firebreak pose no threat. The voices are calm, portending no imminent danger. No one is shouting, "Fire!" Surely there is no cause for alarm.

The environment on our side of the firebreak may appear fairly normal. We get up in the morning and take our children to school or go to our jobs. We go to church, we go to restaurants, we go to ball games and take vacations. We put out a few brush fires, but we can almost forget that there is a dangerous fire brewing. Life is good, and we are rather comfortable. But the fire is out there, and it will take its toll.

Even a green tree dries and withers if a forest fire draws too near, and its "kindling temperature" will be lowered. Even a faithful Christian may change his opinion about what is right and what is wrong when the raging fire of immorality and spiritual decline roars close by. Our respect for God's Word may be eroded by what we hear the world saying. Merely the influence of a sinful world may sway our

> *A fire goes in whatever direction the wind blows.*

thinking and weaken our resolve. A fire goes in whatever direction the wind blows. We will need to be vigilant if we are to avoid going with it.

Even before the flames invade the green side of the firebreak, the heat from their influence can wither our vitality. David mentioned in Psalm 32:4, "...*my strength was sapped as in the heat of summer.*" He was describing the effect of heat upon the human body. Heat drains away our energy, and we may experience malaise and apathy. Our own inner fire may be quenched while that blaze across the firebreak gains momentum.

One aspect of the word "sapping" indicates secretly or covertly undermining something. Our convictions may be subtly undermined by the mere existence of the fire of immorality and spiritual decline. Just the fact that so many normal and intelligent people around us find sin to be acceptable may weaken our conviction about it.

The survivor of the restaurant fire prepared herself for any future fire, and it is interesting that her preparation could well parallel what Christians might do as they live with the threat of a dangerous inferno of a different kind. She said that we should always be aware and knowledgeable of our environment.

Christians benefit by understanding why the world would accept moral decay. Man embraces sin because Satan is alive, well, and quite capable of convincing man that he will make him happy and prosperous. Satan tries the same approach with us that he used on Jesus. In Matthew 4:8 we read, *"Again, the devil took him to a very high mountain and showed him all the kingdoms of the world and their splendor. All this will I give you, he said, if you will bow down and worship me."* Jesus resisted, but man has always had trouble resisting the devil's offer.

What is mankind hoping to accomplish in living by its own rules? Man wants to have a rewarding life and to be respected; yet most of all, he has a deep yearning for eternal life. These are some of the most basic needs of man. So, in the final analysis, man really wants what God is offering, but he has difficulty recognizing that fact.

Sinners find themselves trying very hard to look as if they are having a wonderful time. But if such a life were really so great, they wouldn't have to work so hard to prove it. At the end of the day, they find themselves still searching for something that will make them happy. How foolish Christians would be to allow themselves to be drawn like moths to the fire of moral decay and spiritual decline! Yet, most of us have at least some inclination to be a moth.

If we find ourselves rationalizing God's clear teachings in order to accommodate the opinions espoused by the media and the world, we can know that the heat of that fire has sapped our conviction. When a false philosophy of life is seen and heard repeatedly, it begins to sound true. It is unlikely that most of us hear God's message as often as we hear the doctrine of the world. That is a clear danger sign! We must never depend upon the world to reinforce our godly convictions. It won't happen!

We need to have such joyous conviction that our influence reduces the fire to smoke. It is our steady conviction and joy that can revitalize dry stubble and cause green trees to replace darkened stumps.

Just as Lise Bohannon prepares herself to survive any future fire, so we need to shore up our resolve to survive the fire of moral decay in our land. Perhaps we could take steps to be sure that we hear from God often enough to compete with the media. We can play good CDs or audiotapes of either Christian music or lectures. There are tapes of the entire Bible available. So, if we can't read the entire Bible through in a year, perhaps we can listen through it in a year.

> *We must never depend upon the world to reinforce our godly convictions. It won't happen!*

Many wise parents ration television for their children. Why not ration it for adults in the family as well? We are able to control the frequency with which we are pounded with false messages.

Limiting exposure to an unwholesome environment can drastically change the way we think about God and His will for us.

The fire survivor said that she further prepares herself against fire by carrying a small flashlight when she is in unfamiliar surroundings. She knows that light will be required in order to find her way out of the darkness.

We also need light to find our way through the darkness. The Lord is our light, and He makes our way clear. If we carry His Word in our hearts, we will always be able to find our way—no matter how thick the smoke.

The psalmist wrote in Psalm 119:105, "*Your word is a lamp unto my feet and a light for my path.*" Again, in Psalm 119:130, he said, "*The unfolding of your words gives light; it gives understanding to the simple.*" Such words remind us that the messages from the Lord were meant to guide us in our decision-making process. Those messages enable us to make better choices—choices that keep us out of danger zones. It is God's Word that re-enforces our conviction—not the world.

> *It is God's Word that reinforces our conviction—not the world.*

SINGEING SOURS OUR INFLUENCE

If the flames of a fire actually swipe us, people will notice. The eyebrows are singed—or perhaps gone. The hair on one's head may also be singed, and even the skin could be scorched. We certainly don't want to let a fire get that close!

The most emphatic advice given by the survivor of the restaurant fire was an urgent admonition to respond quickly. If we hope to avoid regressing to the stage of being singed by the world's raging fire of immorality and spiritual decline, we will need to respond quickly. Scripture

> *There is something about doing the right thing that keeps hope alive in our hearts.*

used the word "flee" to describe a quick response to temptation. In I Corinthians 6:18, Paul urged Christians to *"flee sexual immorality."*

The Old Testament showed us two contrasting examples of men who needed to flee, lest they be singed by the fire of immorality. In the familiar story of Joseph found in Genesis 39, we read of Potiphar's wife *"taking notice"* of Joseph. She tried to entice him to betray both his heavenly Father and his earthly master. But Joseph replied, *"My master has withheld nothing from me except you, because you are his wife. How then could I do such a wicked thing and sin against God?"* The next time Potiphar's wife approached him, Joseph ran from the house. It is important to notice that fundamental to Joseph's decision to resist sin was his commitment not to *"sin against God"* (Genesis 39:9). And even though standing for his principles landed him in prison, he didn't seem to regret his decision. There is something about doing the right thing that keeps hope alive in our hearts.

The man who failed to flee was Samson. Samson was born to be set apart to God—a Nazarite. Christians have that in common with Samson; they are "born again" to be set apart to God. In Judges 14, we read that the Spirit of the Lord came upon Samson, and Samson was made physically strong in order to work God's purpose for him. In spite of all that God did through him, Samson walked too close to the fire. He was physically strong, but he had a very noticeable weakness for unprincipled women of the world. He married a Philistine woman, who betrayed him by revealing to the Philistines the answer to his riddle. Later he fell in love with Delilah. She repeatedly tried to learn the secret of his strength in order to help his enemies to capture him. He repeatedly gave her false answers, and she tested each answer. Although certainly singed by Delilah's schemes, Samson still couldn't bring himself to flee.

Sin is a seductive potion. Today, many people become entangled in immoral affairs, and nothing can convince them that they should flee. A father or mother may desert precious children and cling tenaciously to some new lover. Friends and family members are dismayed by such irrational behavior. No one can understand such conduct, because it is unreasonable to forfeit everything for a person who is so unprincipled that she would become involved with someone who is married. There are many "Samsons" today—they may have certain strengths, but morality is not one of them.

Samson's conduct would have been noticeably irrational to anyone except himself. Almost any logical person would have fled after Delilah's first betrayal. That would have been enough to at least singe the eyebrows. But Samson stayed until he lost his hair! Judges 16:20 said, *"And he did not know that the Lord had left him."* At that point he had not yet been physically blinded, but he had been emotionally blinded by his lust. Eventually, the Philistines destroyed his eyesight forever. His principles had been sapped by his obsession with lust, and his respect and influence were singed by conduct unworthy of a judge of Israel.

Christians are sometimes drawn to the idols of this world. Our principles are not sapped just because we are tempted. We lose our conviction when we repeatedly walk too close to the fire. Satan knows our weak spots—pride, greed, lust, and many others. If we spend too much time near the fire, we will likely be singed. We will do things unworthy of God's people, and our influence will be eroded. Others will see that our eyebrows are singed—even if we are not aware.

SEARING DEADENS FEELING

Allowing sin to become a way of life will dull our sensitivity to it. One meaning of the word "sear" is to cauterize or brand with a hot iron; it also means to become callous and without feeling. We live in a time when sin is paraded before us daily, and it is adorned as pleasure, power, and beauty. It smiles at us seductively from the television or movie screen. We see it so frequently that we are not always shocked by it. Perhaps we are at risk of losing our innocence.

Searing or cauterizing doesn't happen while the heat of the fire is at a distance. It happens when that hot iron contacts the skin and firmly presses against it. In I Timothy 4:1, 2, Paul said, *"The Spirit clearly says that in later times some will abandon the faith and follow deceiving spirits and things taught by demons. Such teachings come through hypocritical liars whose consciences have been seared as with a hot iron."*

Searing happens when our flirtation with sin becomes a serious romance. Perhaps we join the community of sinners or we indulge without any restraint in our own personal private sin. Eventually, sin doesn't look so sinful anymore. We demand that God be more understanding of our frailties and needs. In fact, we decide that God doesn't really mind so much that we sin.

> *Eventually, sin doesn't look so sinful anymore.*

The feeling is gone; the conscience is seared. Scripture said that there is a point at which God may let the sinner go. In Romans 1:21, Paul said, *"For although they knew God, they neither glorified him nor gave thanks to Him."* Paul was describing a searing process. In verse 24, he said, *"Therefore God gave them over in the sinful desires of their hearts to sexual impurity for the degrading of their bodies with one another. They exchanged the truth of God for a lie and worshipped and served created things rather than the Creator."*

A Christian reaches this stage when his conviction has gone beyond being sapped and singed. Those first stages are dangerous, but when our hearts are seared, our genuine respect for God is gone. We have a serious love affair with the ways of the world. In II Thessalonians 2:11, Paul wrote, *"For this reason God sends them a strong delusion so that they will believe the lie and so that all will be condemned who have not believed the truth."* Such passages press the urgency that we live our convictions. We dare not try to demote God in order to accommodate our own desires, lest we find ourselves seared.

> *. . . when our hearts are seared, our genuine respect for God is gone.*

Battling the raging fire has always been a part of remaining committed, convicted, and faithful to Christ. Evil lurks nearby, awaiting the opportunity to defeat us. In Matthew 12:43-45, Jesus told a parable about a man who managed to rid himself of an unclean spirit. The man then cleaned and got his house in order. One might think that was a story with a happy ending. But Jesus went on to say that the unclean spirit roamed around for a while and came back. Finding the house clean and spacious, he moved back in and brought seven other spirits more evil than himself. Verse 45 said, *"So the last state was worse than the first."* Evil can be chased away, but we will always have to battle it.

Christians will find it necessary to do more than oppose evil. It is not enough to avoid the fires of temptation. We must actively engage in doing good and honoring God. Some of us are good, but the question is, "Good for WHAT?" When evil comes to our door, it should find a house so crowded with good works that there is no more room.

In I Timothy 6:11, Paul wrote to Timothy saying, *"But you, man of God, flee all this* (evil) *and pursue righteousness, godliness, faith, endurance and gentleness."* Paul didn't just urge Timothy to flee; he cautioned him to do something positive. We tend to always be on the defensive. Our convictions solidify when we go on the offensive, sweeping forward with kindness to the hurting, giving to the needy, and sharing our hope of salvation.

The evil that is in our world today is not new. There have been times when it was possibly worse. Christians will not likely drive all sin from the secular community. But God has equipped us with tools to cut the firebreak. His Spirit living in us will help us to be holy—set apart to Him. The whole Christian community is weakened when one Christian fails to live faithfully. The firebreak exists only because of our conviction and commitment to the teachings of Christ.

With the Lord on our side of the firebreak, nothing can keep us from surviving and thriving in times like these.

EMOTIONS THAT MAKE OR BREAK

"He will have no fear of bad news; his heart is steadfast, trusting in the Lord."

Psalm 112:7

People who are in the business of fighting fires know that certain materials and substances have a much lower "kindling temperature" than others. Dry twigs and underbrush will ignite more quickly because oxygen is able to unite with them rapidly. Oxygen cannot unite so rapidly with the trunk of a green tree, and such a tree ignites only when its temperature is extremely elevated. That level of heat is called "kindling temperature." But a tree that is not healthy will ignite much more quickly.

As the raging fire of spiritual decline and immorality roars in our direction, its heat threatens to move us to "kindling temperature." We find ourselves in a very vulnerable condition. If we are not strong and stable, our response to the fire may look more like that of the world than like Jesus. We may begin having more doubt about our godly position, because there are fewer people who hold that position. We may even question whether we are being radical.

In that case, we might suspect that we are not a healthy tree—perhaps we are about to reach our "kindling temperature." Perhaps the insects of ungodliness are eating away our protective bark. For us, the danger comes not because of our indignation about immorality in our land, but that we might ourselves become a part of that ungodly conduct. As trees on the green side of the firebreak, our response to life's injustices should not be the same as that of dry stubble and underbrush.

Dr. Viktor Frankl once said, "It does not matter what we expect from life. It is what life expects from us. We need not go about searching for the meaning of life. It is life that will question us and search out of what we are made." When the forces of evil spread like a forest fire, life will soon test our mettle! Our response to unfavorable conditions can speak volumes about who we really are. We glorify God when the world can see us responding with strength and stability. It is unlikely that we can be spiritually strong if we are emotionally unstable.

Emotions are mental and physical sensations that we see manifested through our reaction to various circumstances. When heat grows intense, even a fresh, green tree may be susceptible to a fiery eruption. Our emotions are complex, and they range from love to hate—even when applied to the same person or subject. In fact, they are not even very consistent much of the time. For instance, a travel agent once said that a lady who was one of his clients called and asked him to arrange a vacation for her and several of her friends. She said, "I want you to find us some place far away from civilization. And be sure that it is close to a good shopping center!"

> *It is unlikely that we can be spiritually strong if we are emotionally unstable.*

Our emotions are not very dependable and may send unwise messages. They tend to follow our circumstances as they go from positive to negative—then from negative to positive. We may have a couple of weeks when things go smoothly. Then there will be a fender-bender, a family member gets sick, or we didn't get the promotion. That is normal life. Life is not perfect; it never has been.

Jesus' life spanned only slightly more than thirty years, but He too had to grapple with both negatives and positives of life on earth. He certainly experienced opposition to His principles. We remember the glorious day of His baptism when the Spirit of God descended upon Him like a dove. But what happened next? Satan came along and bombarded Him with temptations.

The crowds would flock to Him for healing. Then the priests and Pharisees would be plotting to kill Him.

There was that majestic moment as He experienced the Triumphal Entry with palm leaves and cheering crowds. Then He was betrayed, arrested, and executed.

> *In this life, we need not expect our stability to come from our circumstances.*

In this life, we need not expect our stability to come from our circumstances. It is normal to have positive experiences at times and negative ones at other times. As the saying goes, "chicken one day—feathers the next!" We can expect the unexpected, the unsettling, and the irritating.

The question to ask is, "What did Jesus do when the raging fire of Satan roared in His direction?" How did He manage to stay so committed to His ministry?

OUR SOURCE OF POWER

Through Scripture we can watch Jesus' demeanor as unpleasant circumstances continued to pursue Him. We know that He had normal human emotions, but what we see is a man who was steady and stable. What gave Him the courage and confidence to maintain spiritual and emotional stability, regardless of His circumstances?

> *Jesus knew His Source of power very well.*

There could be only one answer to that question— Jesus knew His Source of power very well. Jesus prayerfully shifted the heat of life's difficulties from His own shoulders to the able shoulders of the Father. It refreshed His spirit and renewed His commitment.

We sometimes feel the heat of the approaching fire and quiver. The trees on the green side of the firebreak could benefit from cooling contact with the Living Water. That water keeps us below "kindling temperature." If we don't have access to that stabilizing force, even the green trees may burst into flames. If we want the kind of stability that Jesus showed us, we must depend upon the Living Water.

> *Trust will prevent spontaneous combustion of our emotions.*

The only stability there is to be had in this world is our trust in the Lord whose promises never fail.

What do we mean when we say that our faith gets us through crisis? It doesn't matter whether it is a small brush fire or a raging fire; our confidence in God to supply the "living water" will keep us cool. Trust will prevent spontaneous combustion of our emotions. Without that trust we will not have genuine stability and commitment. Psalm 73:26 said, *"My flesh and my heart may fail, but God is the strength of my heart."*

We would like to have that steady stability that we saw in Jesus. We would like to be resilient and tenacious in the face of trials. Possibly we don't realize that we are equipped by God to survive the heat of the encroaching fire. In II Peter 1:3, the writer said, *"His divine power has given us everything we need for life and godliness."* Because His Spirit lives in His people, we have everything that we need in order to cope with our difficulties and life's injustices. But we must be careful that we quench the *right fire!* There is a tendency to quench the Spirit within, and thus weaken our chances for survival.

A SPIRIT OF FEARFULNESS

Paul encouraged Timothy to recognize the strengths that were his because of the Spirit. In II Timothy 1, he said, *"For God did not give us a spirit of timidity"* (meaning fearfulness). Quite the contrary! God calls us to courageousness! He calls us to have courage—not because we are invincible—but because He is!

The "spirit of timidity" that Paul said God does not give His people is a spirit of fearfulness. Fear is not a Christian virtue. If we have a spirit of fearfulness, it did

> *If we have a spirit of fearfulness, it did not come from God.*

not come from God. When life searches us, will it find that we are fearful?

We may fear many things in addition to spiritual decline. Fear debilitates us as we worry about health problems so much that we will not even go to the doctor. The doctor might say, "It is malignant." We worry about the safety or behavior of our children. We fret over finances. We even worry about our married children, and then our grandchildren.

We fear how others view us. We fear being embarrassed, and we even fear criticism. We fear certain things going wrong in our country or perhaps the church. The list is endless.

Belonging to God, we do not need to worry or fear the days to come. We can have courage to face unpleasant, unwanted circumstances if we are conscious that His Spirit lives in us. Our "kindling temperature" will never be reached if we maintain confidence and stability.

So, in the passage in II Timothy 1, Paul was preparing Timothy emotionally for his ministry by saying, *"For God did not give us a spirit of timidity, but a spirit of power, of love and of self-discipline."* These are characteristics that Paul knew would serve Timothy well when life searched him and questioned of what he was made. Let us examine what the Spirit has given us to equip us for a time when there is a raging fire.

A SPIRIT OF POWER

First, Paul mentioned that we have been given a spirit of power. Power is something that many people in our culture desire, because they view it as leverage, influence, or the ability to control others. That was not what Paul meant when he used the word, "power."

> ". . . being strengthened with all power according to his glorious might so that you may have great endurance and patience."
> — Colossians 1:11

Paul often spoke of this "power" in his writings. It is the same "power" of which he spoke in Ephesians 1:19, "...His incomparably great power for us who believe. That power is like the working of his mighty strength." It is a strength for us when there is a raging fire or perhaps when there is a small brush fire. It is what we need when we lose a job, our child is in trouble, or when the doctor says, "It is malignant."

In Colossians 1:11, Paul wrote, "...being strengthened with all power according to his glorious might so that you may have great endurance and patience." Now we can see the real value of this power. It gives us tenacity and patience to keep going or get back up even in the face of a whole string of adversities. Sometimes people encounter not just one fire, but multiple fires. Jesus endured numerous hardships as He carried out His mission here on earth. The apostle Paul likewise suffered loss of friends and family. He was imprisoned, beaten, and shipwrecked. Both Jesus and Paul displayed for us the strength that God infuses into His people. In Romans 8:26, Paul said,

"The Spirit helps us in our weakness." We certainly have all kinds of weaknesses. This spirit of "power" allows us to overcome our tendency to be controlled by the fear of this life's problems.

Paul even prayed about this spirit of power in Ephesians 3:16, *"I pray that out of his glorious riches, he may strengthen you with power."* It is very encouraging to know that God has given us a measure of His strength.

We don't know what the years ahead may bring. But we do know that adversity has its limitations. It can do many things, but it cannot take away our hope. We can give away our hope, but no one can take it from us. Such knowledge should reduce that fear or timidity, which Paul said does not come from God. That is why Jesus said in Luke 12:4, 5, *"Fear not him who can kill the body and after that can do not more. I tell you whom you should fear. Fear him who after killing the body has the power to throw you into hell. Yes, I tell you, fear him."*

There is emotional strength and stability in being able to put this life in its proper perspective. It will give us endurance and patience to see us through the adversity brought by the raging fire of immorality and spiritual decline in our land.

A SPIRIT OF LOVE

Paul told Timothy that the second characteristic which had been infused was the spirit of love. There is something stabilizing about turning our attention outward and caring about the needs of others. It gives life meaning and purpose. Scripture said, "God is love," so if His Spirit lives in us, we should have the capacity to love people. Caring about others takes some of the momentum out the fire of worldliness that threatens us.

Jesus went about showing His genuine love for people. He focused on others even as brush fires broke out all around Him. In I Thessalonians 3:12 Paul said, *"May the Lord make your love increase and overflow for each other and for everyone else, just as ours does for you."* It was always important to Paul that our love be out of a pure heart. In I Timothy 1:5, Paul said, *"The aim of our charge is love that issues from a pure heart."* In Romans 12:9 he said, *"Love must be sincere."* Paul meant that Timothy should genuinely care about people, not just talk about love but put it into practice.

Like Timothy, we are God's instruments. God's love is poured out on people, but He uses us to hold the pitcher. If we don't really care about people, there will sometimes be love in our pitchers, and sometimes there will be nothing in our pitchers—depending on how busy we are with our own brush fires.

> *God's love is poured out on people, but He uses us to hold the pitcher.*

Sometimes we decide not to help others because we suspect that they may be responsible for their own brush fire. We conclude that such reckless people don't deserve our help. Sometimes, when people need support, they feel only our judgment. That is how Job felt when his "supporters" were not inclined to help put out the fire. In Job 12:5 he said, "*Men at ease have contempt for misfortune as the fate of those whose feet are slipping.*" Job was made to feel as if he had done something that caused his misfortune. Whether our judgment is accurate or not, being judgmental is never comforting to someone in crisis. Jesus put out fires for many people who didn't deserve His love.

Loving people diminishes the heat so that we ourselves don't reach that dangerous "kindling temperature." To maintain an emotionally and spiritually stable life, we must have purpose. If we are to be like Jesus, our major purpose will have to do with caring about people.

Dr. Viktor Frankl said to his fellow prisoners in the death camp at Auschwitz: "No matter how deplorable the circumstances in which one finds himself, life still expects something from him." He said that some of those prisoners went out each day with purpose. They would go about encouraging fellow prisoners or telling stories to young children in order to distract them from their frightening conditions. He found that those who best endured that death camp were those whose focus made the difference. It was those lives that had purpose. Having purpose eroded their fear and anxiety and gave them stability.

Scripture teaches us that no matter what our circumstances, God can work His purpose through us. It doesn't matter whether we are rich or poor, ill or well, in crisis or peace. Purposeful lives are usually stable lives, and helping God to pour out His love upon people gives our lives purpose.

The passage in I Timothy 1:7, written by Paul to Timothy, should teach us that through the Spirit living in us we can have strength for our own trials and love for helping other people in their trials.

A SPIRIT OF SELF-DISCIPLINE

The third characteristic that the Spirit living in us supplies is self-discipline. What feels like the right thing to do is not necessarily the right thing. The easiest and most natural thing to do is often the wrong thing to do.

Emotions send us wrong signals sometimes. For example, if our clothing catches fire, we will tend to run. Running has the effect of fanning the flames, thus supplying more oxygen to burn. The experts say that we should stop, drop, and roll in order to smother the fire. It is not the natural thing to do—in fact, it requires a great deal of self-discipline. God created us to have emotions, but those emotions should be servants—not our rulers.

When Peter spoke to Christians in II Peter 1:5, 6, he was giving them a formula for being able to *"participate in the divine nature* (that is, to be more like Jesus) *and escape the corruption in the world caused by evil desires"* (Showing that evil, unholy emotions are present, even in Christians.). Evil is in the world because evil desires are not controlled. So, Peter told those Christians, *"For this reason, make every effort to add to your faith goodness, to goodness knowledge, to knowledge self-control..."*

We see from that passage the role that self-discipline plays in building Christian character that resembles Jesus. Without self-discipline our emotions and our desires will guide our judgment about moral issues. That firebreak between the raging fire and us can begin to shrink. We make decisions daily about whether we will repeat gossip, whether we will be honest, and so on. It is a tug of war every day! Without self-discipline, you know which side will win!

> *Without self-discipline our emotions and our desires will guide our judgment about moral issues.*

Paul spoke of his own efforts of self-discipline in I Corinthians 9:26, 27: *"I do not run like a man running aimlessly. I do not fight like a man beating the air. No, I beat my body and make it my slave so that after I have preached to others, I myself will not be disqualified for the prize."*

Unhealthy attitudes and unholy desires come to us without having been invited. Feelings of resentment seem to surface for one reason or another. Certainly, feelings of anger and a deep-seated need for vengeance roll over us like flames driven by a strong wind, destroying our sense of better judgment. Such emotions do not reflect Jesus or His steady and thoughtful response to those who opposed Him.

Anger and a desire for vengeance reflect that fire raging out-of-control on the other side of the firebreak. Anger destroys its owner. All that a raging fire leaves behind is a darkened, destroyed forest. To feel the heat of anger may be normal, but to embrace it is deadly and self-destructive.

Even our seemingly normal passions, emotions, or feelings require our diligence to keep them under control. The fact is, God called His people to a higher way of thinking and behaving, and it is a way that does not come naturally! That is why Timothy was told that self-discipline must be practiced. It is a vital ingredient as we try to implement a style of thinking and behaving that reflects Jesus and brings Him honor. There was no glory to Jesus if Timothy spewed bitterness and anger every time he was mistreated. Neither is there honor for Jesus if we spew anger when we are mistreated.

Philippians 2:5 said, *"Your attitude should be the same as that of Christ."* Perhaps it would be a worthy exercise to pay attention to our own thoughts and ask ourselves whether there is any similarity between our style of thinking and that of Jesus. If someone harms us by words or deeds, hurts our feelings, deceives us, or threatens us, can we pause and ask, "What would Jesus think in this situation?" "What would He say?" The Scriptures are replete with examples of what He would think and do. Jesus prayed for His enemies, *"Father, forgive them, for they do not know what they are doing."* Luke 23:34

> *There was no glory to Jesus if Timothy spewed bitterness and anger every time he was mistreated.*

RESPONDING TO THE RAGING FIRE

As Dr. Viktor Frankl watched human conduct in that death camp at Auschwitz, he saw that the horrible conditions brought out the best in some people. It brought out the worst in others. Some people became almost like animals, while others became very caring and benevolent toward their fellow sufferers. He learned much about human behavior in crisis. He concluded that the answers to most of our problems in life are two-fold:

1.   Right action and right conduct—always do the right thing. That is, try to possess a sense of right and wrong and have the character to follow those principles. Those who steadily stayed the course day by day at Auschwitz seemed to be those who were stable emotionally and spiritual-

> *"Even in darkness light dawns for the upright."*
> *—Psalm 112:4*

ly. They seemed to have a more positive focus. Scripture put it this way in Psalm 112:4, *"Even in darkness light dawns for the upright."* Responding to the heat as Jesus did will renew our strength and brighten our hope.

Was Scripture saying, "If it feels good, it must be right?" Absolutely not! It was saying those who do what is right cannot be defeated. They cannot be stripped of their hope. There is always a beam of light—even in darkness.

So if we do what is right—not what we rationalize to be right—then our circumstances can never overcome us.

2.   Take responsibility to find right answers for our problems instead of becoming hopeless. It is much easier

to complain about the heat, rather than making the effort to extinguish the fire.

One of my favorite stories is about a young man who had always wanted to be a preacher. It had been his childhood dream, but he had a problem. He stuttered!

He went to doctors, therapists and counselors, but he continued to stutter. He became angry with God, because He would not heal him of his stuttering.

Finally, he went to see another counselor. He sat in the counselor's office and raged against God. When he finished, the counselor said, "Jim, if God were to come into this room and say to you, 'I have one thing I want you to do for me with your life.' What would you say?" Jim quickly responded, "You know that I would do it!"

The counselor said, "Well, God has already spoken, and He has said to you, 'I want you to live your life radiantly, gloriously, in an exemplary way—as a STUTTERER'!"

The counselor said that he did not see Jim again for a long time, but the next time he saw Jim he was preaching. Oh, not the way he had always dreamed. He was preaching to the deaf, using sign language. It did not matter at all that he stuttered.

Jim had gone out and found the answer for his problem. Life has a way of not going like we dreamed it would. We experience everything from disappointment to disaster—from "bad hair days" to outright tragedy. We have to be committed enough to take responsibility for finding right answers.

Jesus gave everything in His effort to rein in Satan's flames of destruction. Right answers for us will be found by emulating His life.

With the fire of immorality and spiritual decline roaring in the distance, will God's people merely be heard complaining about the heat, filled with self-pity or maybe just consumed with self? When life brings unpleasant, unwanted circumstances, we can allow them to destroy us body and soul—or we can rise above them. Scripture clearly shows us that adversity can make us stronger.

In I Peter 1:6, 7, Peter was speaking to suffering Christians, when he said:

Though now for a little while you may have had to suffer grief in all kinds of trials. These have come so that your faith—of greater worth than gold, which perishes even though refined by fire— may be proved genuine and may result in praise, honor and glory when Jesus Christ is revealed.

> *Scripture clearly shows that adversity can make us stronger.*

Peter seemed to say that trials are allowed in order to refine our faith. He also seemed to recognize that our faith is so fragile that it tends to perish even though it is refined by fire.

In Romans 5:3, Paul said, "*Suffering produces perseverance.*" It has been said that faith is like a tea bag. It isn't worth much until it has been through a little hot water.

God's people tend to grow best in the heat. We have enjoyed decades of pampered Christianity, which has tended to weaken rather than strengthen. In the first few chapters of the book of Acts, we see the early church settled comfortably in Jerusalem. In Acts 8, those Christians were scattered by persecution. If the church had been a human institution, it would likely have been destroyed at that time. But it belonged to God! Although the church has never been without brush fires, there has never been a fire that could destroy it. God's people will survive, and perhaps they may even thrive in a time of raging fire.

TRYING TO BE SELFLESS
IN A SELFISH WORLD

"For everyone who exalts himself will be humbled, and he who humbles himself will be exalted"
Luke 14:11

The theater was dark, and the performers were on stage before a finely coifed and gowned audience. During the last half of the performance, someone began to faintly smell smoke. The more that he sniffed, the more certain he became that the theater was on fire. He stood up and frantically screamed, "Fire! Fire!"

The startled audience sprang from their seats, trying to get to an exit. They were pushing and shoving, and some were actually fighting. Anyone who fell was trampled by the stampede. No consideration was given to anyone else. The well being of others had no place in this kind of mentality. It was all about self!

> *When a culture begins to turn away from God, it usually will substitute something in His place.*

More than one hundred people died in that tragedy. Perhaps the greatest tragedy of all was that the fire was not serious—certainly not life-threatening.

In a world threatened by the fire of moral and spiritual decline, once again we see this selfish mentality. When a culture begins to turn away from God, it usually will substitute something in His place. In Romans 1:22, 23, Paul said, "*Although they claimed to be wise, they became fools and exchanged the glory of the immortal God for images made to look like mortal man and birds and animals and reptiles.*" Every pagan culture seems to have followed that exact order of idolatry. Today, the world has again attempted to elevate man to the level of a god, and perhaps we are even seeing signs of the next stages of idolatrous decline.

Man chooses his religion according to what makes him feel comfortable and whatever makes the fewest demands of him. When man is elevated, God is always diminished. His Word and His will become irrelevant, because pleasing man is more important.

Selfishness was right at the center of the fall of man in the Garden of Eden, and it has been a weakness of mankind throughout history. Almost every sin of man has its roots in the sin of selfishness.

When the serpent set his trap for Eve, he seized upon the choicest fruit to offer, and it wasn't just the fruit of a tree. It was something that appealed to her selfish side. In Genesis 3:5. He said, "*When you eat of it . . . you will be like God.*" He was not suggesting that she would be righteous like God. He meant that she would know everything like God. Omniscience and power sounded really good!

In today's culture, men aren't so concerned about being righteous like God—they want to be gods! They want power, prestige, and happiness. It is downright politically incorrect to be deprived of happiness.

> *Almost every sin of man has its roots in the sin of selfishness.*

John Stossel did a documentary for ABC Television on the subject of happiness. His research indicated that our ancestors didn't expect to be happy in this life. For them, it was enough to look forward to happiness in heaven. Not so today! It seems that everyone today has a *right* to happiness. How did we get so far down this road?

For one thing, each generation began desiring that its offspring have a better life than their parents had. It probably was not difficult to convince the offspring that indeed they should have a better life.

Therefore, when we were children, we began to dream dreams about a wonderfully happy life. Little boys didn't go about dreaming that some day they may have to work two jobs. They dreamed of being a star athlete or the CEO of a large corporation.

Little girls dreamed about tea parties and pretty dresses. They dreamed that as they grew up they would meet a handsome prince, have a wonderful romance and get married. The marriage would be even more wonderful than the courtship. Then they would have children—not just any children! They would have perfect children—children who would never disappoint them or embarrass them.

And, of course, there would be no serious illness. Perhaps we knew that eventually we would die—but it would be peacefully in our sleep at about age 99.

That is not real life—it is fantasy. Real life is usually sprinkled with various kinds of trouble—even tragedy. But such difficulties are hardly ever expected—and they certainly were never included in our daydreams. It is no wonder that adversity tends to wield a "knock out" punch for us. It was never supposed to happen to us!

It was never supposed to happen to us!

That raging fire of moral and spiritual decline will likely touch us personally in some way. It may cause us to be so self-centered that we trample others who happen to get in our way. No matter how much we might like to have life go our way, we will experience many disappointments and even disasters. Many different factors will influence how we respond when things go wrong. Our obsession with self will be a major factor affecting our response. Like the people in that dark theater, we may forget all morals and act in our own best interest.

> *Our focus on self is often an integral part of our response to anything pleasant or unpleasant that happens to us.*

IT'S ALL ABOUT ME

Our focus on self is often an integral part of our response to anything pleasant or unpleasant that happens to us. If something unpleasant happens, the first question we ask is, "Why me?" Often we think, "How unfair this is to me!" We live in a culture that has a fixation upon self. Walk into any bookstore, and you will see a whole section devoted to self-help. There are books about self-image, self-awareness, self-affirmation, and self-fulfillment.

Even Christians may sit in worship services pondering their own personal affairs. We tend to be so absorbed with our own lives that it is very challenging to put aside our thoughts about what we will be doing next week or about the ball game that comes on television right after church services. Christians may struggle with this matter of selfishness just as much as the outside world.

Unbelievers, however, tend to shock us with their blatantly selfish acts. In newspapers we read about women and men who abandon their families in order to find self-fulfillment. It seems that self comes before commitment to a spouse or concern for children. I have a large folder of newspaper articles about people who have done unthinkably selfish acts.

Some stories tell about young women who become pregnant out of wedlock. Pregnancy is a terrible inconvenience for them personally. So if they don't abort the pregnancy, they have the baby, throw it in the trash can and return to the dance. Other stories tell of mothers who leave a child in a hot car while they go into an air-conditioned salon to have their nails done. Of course, the child dies.

People are absorbed with self, and selfishness is a sign of immaturity. So when disappointment comes, it is overwhelming. Why? It is because we view everything from the perspective of how it affects me. Such an attitude makes for a miserable, never-satisfied life—which explains why so many people are miserable.

> We don't often recognize our own selfishness.

I WANT IT MY WAY

There is probably no aspect of the raging fire that Christians have embraced so much as that of selfishness.

We don't often recognize our own selfishness; we just assume that everything is supposed to revolve around our whims. Such an atti-tude can damage or destroy most relationships. Concern for our own needs blindfolds us to the needs of others. Even in the

> *Over a period of time, selfishness can destroy a marriage relationship.*

church, disagreements may arise because so many people want things to go their own way. In family relationships, arguments begin over petty opinions. If I want to spend my vacation at the seashore, the rest of the family would be totally insensitive to disagree. In the marriage relation-ship, the self-centered partner will not likely consider whether his or her actions may cause hurt or inconven-ience to the other partner. Over a period of time, selfish-ness can destroy a marriage relationship.

In other relationships, selfishness shoves its own will into the lives of friends and even strangers. There is the idea that people are supposed to conduct themselves in a manner that satisfies me or meets my standards. They had better agree with me on every issue, otherwise they will be on my "most disliked" list.

Selfishness causes us to have an ego that is never quite satisfied. Everyone benefits from compliments, but the person who is really selfish will be depressed if people don't heap praise upon him. They want to be credited with any little good thing that they do, and could never do a good deed anonymously. These are the ones most likely to be offended if public commendation isn't given.

The family of Teddy Roosevelt said of him, "He wants to be the bride at every wedding and the corpse at every funeral." That graphically describes those who have a deep need to be the center of attention.

Selfish people tend to dominate the conversation and prefer that it be all about themselves and their interests. And if anyone happens to schedule something on the same date as her special event, there will be big trouble! They are prone to vengeance or retaliation of some kind, or at least pouting and anger. If we have let selfishness overtake us, disappointment will overwhelm us and adversity will tend to destroy us. When it is all about "me," we see more negatives, and they impact us on a personal level.

JUST ME AND MY POSSESSIONS

Our value system becomes distorted when we put our own needs and desires ahead of everything else. Like that proverbial moth, we find ourselves fluttering toward the fire. Our attraction to worldly goods and wealth will often be a factor and our finances may actually be affected. Delayed gratification is not a popular concept in our culture, and the selfish person feels that he deserves to have his desires fulfilled immediately. Hardly anyone wants to wait for anything.

It is something that gets totally out of control, like an addiction. I watched a young couple browsing in a store recently. The girl was pregnant, and their conversation saddened me. Obviously, they had overspent their limit on their credit cards and were looking for other ways to buy things. The girl was suggesting that they might try putting some items on her mother's layaway.

Our love affair with worldly goods and money sometimes unnecessarily cause us problems, pain, and depression. The Lord knew just how attached we human beings would get to our worldly possessions. That is why He spoke about that subject as much

> *The Lord knew just how attached we human beings would get to our worldly posssessions.*

as He did. Selfishness is closely related to man's attraction to things. Did you ever notice how many of the parables deal with the subject of our worldly possessions?

In Luke 12:13, 14, there is the story of brothers arguing over their inheritance. Jesus said to them in verse 15, *"Be on your guard against all kinds of greed. A man's life does not consist in the abundance of his possessions."*

In the story of the Rich Man and Lazarus in Luke 16, we see the rich man securing everything but his own soul, and that is what many of us do today.

When we talk about possessions, pride is in the mix. Jesus tried to teach us that we should not obsess to possess. In Matthew 6:25, He said, *"Therefore I tell you, do not worry about your life, what you will eat or drink; or about your body, what you will wear. Is not life more important than food, and the body more important than clothes?"*

In a time of spiritual decline, even Christians may find their priorities out of order. In Colossians 3:5, Paul said that greed is a form of idolatry. We may become so self-centered that we feel resentful toward God when we don't have as much as certain others. If that is our attitude, that raging fire in our culture today has likely contaminated us. We have forgotten to be thankful.

THANKFULNESS BRINGS JOY

In the Old Testament, King David was a man who experienced a plethora of disappointment, pain, and even disaster. Saul stalked him in an effort to kill him. He had countless battles and enemies, and his children were an unthinkable disappointment. In spite of all those unwanted circumstances, it was David who felt God's love so strongly. In some of the Psalms he poured forth his pain to God, but most of them are tributes of praise to a loving God. In Psalm 8:3, he wrote:

"When I consider the heavens, the work of your fingers, the moon and stars which you have set in place, what is man that you are mindful of him?"

Here was David, who had suffered so much adversity, feeling awe and amazement that God cared so much about mankind. He was not asking why God allowed him to have trouble and inconvenience but was wondering why God would be so kind to mere man. He was awed that God would surround him with beauty and give him great honor. It is unusual for man to be able to focus on his blessings while he is in the midst of adversity.

In light of some of David's frailties, we might be surprised that God could call him *"a man after His own heart."* It may have been because David knew how to be grateful.

He felt loved by God because of the blessings that he did have, and he loved God in return.

Most of us tend to focus on what we don't have. We spot every little negative thing in our lives. Rarely do we genuinely remember to be thankful for what we do have. On a cold, rainy night as we snuggle in warm beds, do we reflect on the fact that there are many others who are not so blessed? Or do we lie there thinking, "What has God done for me lately?"

> *Selfish people are not usually thankful people, but thankful people are happy people.*

Selfish people are not usually thankful people, but thankful people are happy people. In David's heart, gratefulness was woven right through the pain.

LET THIS CUP PASS

Most of us are selfish enough to find suffering a very unpopular idea. Even the apostles didn't exactly sign on expecting to suffer. They thought they were getting in on the ground floor of something big. They even argued about which one would be the most important in this new kingdom (Luke 9:46).

When Jesus began showing them that He would suffer many things and eventually be killed, Peter objected vehemently (Mark 8:31, 32). Peter didn't want there to be dishonor, pain, disappointment and shame. Jesus would have to teach selflessness even to these special followers.

So, Jesus responded to Peter, *"Get behind me, Satan."* Very strong language! In no uncertain terms, Jesus was making it clear that suffering would not be removed from the cross.

Eventually, Jesus said to His followers, *"Pick up your cross and follow me."* Like that original cross, our cross will not be without disappointment, heartache, pain, and perhaps even shame. And like those original followers, we too would prefer the honor and the glory, but we might like to take a "pass" on suffering. We are always in the process of learning the selflessness of Jesus.

Lest you think that I am suggesting that we all run out and volunteer for a day of suffering, let me hasten to say that there would probably be something wrong with us if we went around looking for a chance to suffer. There would really be something wrong if we went around trying to cause others to suffer.

Take note that Jesus Himself did not want to drink that cup. In Mark 14:36, the writer portrayed Jesus in the Garden of Gethsemane as the time for the agony drew near, and He prayed, *"Abba Father—all things are possible with you. Take away this cup from me!"* It sounds similar to the prayer that we pray when there is terminal illness. We pray that same prayer when there is business failure or our children disappoint us.

So we see that Jesus wanted a different cup, but the important thing was what He said next. *"Nevertheless not what I will, but what you will."* At that moment, Jesus set for us the supreme example of selfless attitude in adversity. He willingly submitted His own will (I don't want this cup), to the will of God.

In Hebrews 5:8, 9, the writer said, "*Although He was a son, He learned obedience from what He suffered, and once made perfect, He became the source of eternal salvation for all who obey Him.*"

The Greek word for perfect is *teleios,* and can mean more than "without flaw or blemish." In fact, Jesus was already without flaw or blemish. The word *teleios* also means that a thing is perfect when it perfectly carries out the function for which it was designed. Our air conditioners are *teleios* if they cool our houses. Jesus was *teleios* (perfect), because He submitted His will to God and therefore became the sacrifice for the sins of man—which was His purpose.

The opposite of love is not necessarily hate; the opposite of love is selfishness!

What if He had been selfish? The only reason that we have any hope of heaven is that Jesus was willing to drink a cup that He did not want to drink. The opposite of love is not necessarily hate; the opposite of love is selfishness!

There will be times when we are called upon to drink a cup that we don't really want to drink. Can we submit our will without resentment? Can we trust God with our adversity? Or will selfishness be our attitude? Sometimes, it is only through suffering that the Lord can work His purpose through us.

SELFLESSNESS BRINGS JOY

Through His example Jesus was teaching us to be self-less and look to the interest of others. A few years ago a young African-American mother was killed, leaving five young children. There was no one to take the children except her younger brother who was in his early twenties. He had been saving money to go to college. His whole future lay ahead. If he took those children, he would never get his education. He wondered if he would ever be able to marry and have a family of his own.

He decided that he had been given an opportunity to make a difference in the lives of those children. He agreed to take them and just hoped that rearing those children would be as rewarding as life could get. He used his college money to buy a small house. Many people heard about his selflessness and donated money to help. At last report, he was still successfully rearing those children. He had not married nor had he gone to college.

Those who are influenced by Jesus instead of the world will humble themselves to the level of a servant. We should avoid seeking only relationships that can benefit ourselves. A selfless heart will look for ways to serve those who could never repay our kindness. Jesus picked up the broken people and gave them honor. He helped the tax collectors, the Samaritan woman, and even a thief on a cross.

> *We are afraid that a sacrificial life will make us miserable.*

In Romans 12:16, Paul exhorted the church, *". . . be willing to associate with people of low position. Do not be conceited."*

Paul urged Christians to give up their selfishness. In Romans 12:1, he said, *"I urge you brothers, in view of God's mercy, to offer your bodies as living sacrifices, holy and pleasing to God."* But we tend to be so protective of our own rights and privileges that we don't want to give up anything. We are afraid that a sacrificial life will make us miserable. In reality, a selfless, holy way of life will have delightful side effects. It will bless us with good relationships, better health, peace, harmony, and hope. Taking the focus off self translates into happiness!

Too much concern about our own personal interests may cause us to neglect God's work. Our resolve to do what is right may be withered by the influence of the fire of spiritual decline.

WHEN OUR CHILDREN GO ASTRAY

"O Absalom my son, my son."

II Samuel 19:4

It was not our usual Thanksgiving holiday, but we were excited about our trip to the Texas hill country. We were joining another couple for a holiday hunting trip. The hunting lease was on a beautiful, thousand-acre ranch with rolling hills and thick forests. Other ranches of similar size and terrain bordered the ranch.

It was our custom to arise very early—about 4:00 a.m.—get dressed, go out, and sit quietly in a deer blind. Those early morning hours were cold and felt even colder as we sat in the semi-darkness of that deer blind. Our son was eight years old and our daughter was about nine, and they were quite excited about this adventure.

By about 9:00 a.m., we were back at the house enjoying a hearty breakfast. Like most eight-year-olds, Keith finished his breakfast quickly and asked if he could walk down to the road to try to see a deer. Permission was given.

Within a matter of minutes our son had disappeared. We walked around the area calling his name but got no response. Because of the density of the forest, even adults could become lost quite easily while trying to search for this child. So, the men, being more familiar with the terrain, began the search while the women waited anxiously. I felt confident that he would soon be found, but I was sorely mistaken.

After a while, the men returned and called the sheriff. Accustomed to organizing search parties for lost hunters in this area, the sheriff responded quickly. He arrived with his crew of searchers and turned on the siren in his car. He was hoping that Keith would hear the siren and perhaps walk toward the sound. It did not happen.

The sun steadily moved toward the western horizon. Not many hours of daylight remained. Several hours of intense searching brought no success, and no one could forget that thousands of acres surrounded us.

Knowing how difficult this kind of search might be, the sheriff began asking questions of Bob and me. "Did you tell your son not to ever cross a fence?"

"No, you see, we didn't expect him to ever be out of our sight," we sheepishly replied.

"It will soon be dark," said the sheriff. (That thought was foremost in my mind.) "Did you give him matches?" We would never have given him matches because of the danger of forest fires.

"No, you see, we didn't expect...."

"Did he have a warm jacket?"

"No."

"A flashlight?"

"No."

After answering "no" to all those questions about preparation, we felt like really poor parents.

"Well," said the sheriff, "grown men have been lost for days on this acreage. I am going to try to get some helicopter assistance."

My heart sank. I could not bear the thought of my child out there in the dark alone. Soon darkness began closing its ominous cloak around us. My husband was still out there somewhere, searching for his lost son. My job was to stay at the house and pray.

Keith had been missing since about 10:00 a.m., and Bob had been walking constantly since that time. He was weary and his feet were sore, but as he walked, he suddenly found himself in a meadow, clear of trees. In fact, a flock of sheep could be seen in the distance. Thinking that perhaps he heard a voice, Bob stopped and listened. Finally, he decided it must have been the sheep and began walking again. He stopped again. It really sounded like a voice! He began running toward the sound. In the semi-darkness, he could make out the familiar figure.

"Dad!" came the anxious little voice.

"Son, where have you been?" Bob asked, somewhat facetiously.

His face darkened with the tear-stained dirt of his ordeal, Keith looked in disbelief at his Dad. "I've been lost!" he replied. "I've been really lost."

Indeed, he had seen a deer that morning at the road, and he had innocently followed it into the forest. After only a few yards into the forest, all sense of direction was lost—and so was he!

Believe me, we were ready to put the ring on his finger and kill the fatted calf. Our son was lost, but now was found!

Although there was no fire raging in that particular forest at that specific time, one can erupt very quickly in such areas. In our world today, the fires that threaten our children are spotty, igniting in some of the most unexpected places. As parents, we want to protect our children from the pitfalls that await them in the world. We hope that they will grow up knowing God and staying in His family. We try to equip them for the battle that we know they will face as they lose their sweet innocence. We know that they will meet Satan in the desert of temptation. Just as God's Son had to have that encounter, so every son or daughter today will know the enticing call of Satan.

THE DESERT OF TEMPTATION

We pray, "Lord, please protect them when they meet those temptations." We try to think of all the right things to do in order to equip them, but it is a formidable and clever enemy that they are about to meet out there in the desert.

> *Just as God's Son had to have that encounter, so every son or daughter today will know the enticing call of Satan.*

In spite of all efforts, sometimes our children go astray. To the parents who have trained and nurtured those children, such a disaster feels like one of life's cruelest injustices. Can it be fair that you try very hard to prepare your children for the desert, and still they succumb to Satan's enticing wiles? Meanwhile, we may see others who do not seem very concerned about preparing their little ones for life, and those children may grow up and remain faithful.

Schools have typically been the first stop for our children in the desert of temptation. It was where they learned not only reading, writing, and arithmetic, but also social skills—every kind of social skill! Inevitably, some of those skills will not be moral.

In earlier school environments, there was more attention given to right conduct. Some things were wrong, and everybody knew it. There were some children who majored in doing "bad" things, but we knew who those people were, and we knew that we should not join their group.

In today's non-judgmental environment, the lines are more blurred. Even some teachers do not feel the responsibility to maintain high standards of personal conduct. One school was sued recently for trying to fire a teacher who was living with a female to whom he was not married. Sometimes legal constraints seem to favor immorality.

Schools have bought into the idea that every vestige of Christianity must be banished from the school environment. Meanwhile, almost anything else—no matter how unseemly—is acceptable. Children are inundated with vile, immoral language of their peers. They are exposed to frightening and dangerous lifestyles. The climate in many schools is perfect for igniting dry twigs, which may explode into their own raging fire.

It has been said that after about age ten, our children will begin to suspect that their friends are smarter than their parents. Soon after that, they will think that everyone is smarter than their parents.

Concerned parents are beginning to home-school their children. They are putting forth this diligent effort in order to protect their children from a harmful and immoral environment. Studies are beginning to show that home-schooled children are actually ranking higher on standardized tests than children being educated in public schools.

Parents who can financially afford to do so send their children to private religious schools. More than twenty-five years ago, an educator predicted a massive change in the way children would be educated in the United States. It seemed difficult to believe at the time. Now his prediction is coming true, as we watch public education being destroyed.

Perhaps all is not lost, since large numbers of students are beginning to be taught in a better environment. However, far too many children are being lost in the desert of temptation, because they have no choice but to be there.

WHO IS TO BLAME?

A dear Christian friend, who is now a senior citizen, cannot quite find peace in her soul because so many of her family have left the Lord. In her sweet little voice, she said to me recently, "I guess there must be something wrong with my religion, so many of those I love have not remained faithful to the Lord." I had always known that she agonized over that matter. Hoping to ease her pain, I said, "You know, Adam and Eve had the best parent that anyone could have, and they still went astray." I think I saw a small glimmer of consolation in her face.

> *Adam and Eve had the best parent that anyone could have, and they still went astray.*

Ultimately, who is accountable for "lostness"? Is it the parent—or is it the one who chooses to join the world rather than the family of God? Many parents try very hard to influence their children to make right choices, while other parents are not very concerned. Some have said, "No matter how successful I am in life, I will consider myself a failure if my child is lost to the Lord"—thus taking the blame upon themselves.

No matter how diligently the parent may try, it will be the child who finally makes the choice. We are each given the freedom to choose God or reject Him, and God gave that freedom to us. Actually, most parents are very cautious about relinquishing decision-making to their children, because they know the threat of the raging fire.

> *Not only parents, but also all men are accountable to God for their influence.*

There is much that a parent can do to prepare children for the desert of temptation, and the parent is responsible to God for the protection and influence that he gives his children. A passage in Matthew 18:7 says,

Woe to the world because of the things that cause people to sin! Such things must come, but woe to the man through whom they come!

Not only parents but also all men are accountable to God for their influence. Even so, Scripture is very clear that the individual who has chosen sin will answer to God.

In Ezekiel 18, the entire chapter is spent on the question of accountability. It is a chapter that everyone should carefully study. The writer in Ezekiel 18:1 ff. said,

The word of the Lord came to me, "What do you people mean by quoting this proverb about the land of Israel?:

'The fathers eat sour grapes, and their

children's teeth are set on edge?'

As surely as I live, says the Sovereign Lord, you will no longer quote this proverb in Israel. For every living soul belongs to me, the father as well as the son—both alike belong to me. The soul who sins is the one who will die."

There can be no doubt about accountability. The chapter goes on to describe a righteous man, who does everything according to God's decrees, and it says *that* man *"will surely live."* The man has a son who is violent and breaks all decrees. Of the son he says, *"Will such a man live? He will not!"*

Then, there is described the son born to this wicked son—in fact, the grandson of the righteous man. Verse 14 said, *"But suppose this* (wicked) *son has a son who sees all the sins his father commits, and though he sees them, he does not do such things."* In fact, this young man lives righteously in spite of his father's wickedness. The passage said that the righteous son would surely live.

This passage goes to great length to teach that as children grow to the age at which they can discern right from wrong, they are accountable for the choices they make.

Verse 20 concludes, *"The righteousness of the righteous man will be credited to him, and the wickedness of the wicked will be charged against him."*

The Lord Himself acknowledged that righteous parents sometimes have wicked children, and oddly enough, wicked parents sometimes have righteous children. It does happen! Does this passage cause the hearts of righteous parents to feel any comfort when their child has gone astray? Not likely! The only thing that would console that parent would be seeing their child freed from Satan's clutches.

CHILDREN SUFFER CONSEQUENCES OF PARENTS' SINS

Before leaving the subject of responsibility and accountability for children who go astray, we must examine the Scriptures which teach that children do suffer the "natural consequences" of the sins of their fathers. In Numbers 14:18, the writer said, "...*He punishes the children for the sin of the fathers to the third and fourth generation.*" Verse 33 of the same chapter said, "*Your children will be shepherds here (in the desert) for forty years, suffering for your unfaithfulness.*"

The children of wicked parents usually do painfully suffer the consequences of their parents' sins. We regularly read about little children living in filthy conditions, deprived and neglected. We hear about mothers, living out of wedlock, with some creature that abuses her children. Heartbreaking statistics show that a large percentage of such women would sooner give up their children than their lover. Many parents today are addicted to drugs and alcohol and even give such substances to their small children. And raging fire threatens to burn out of control.

A few years ago, I taught Bible to young women who had used both alcohol and other drugs to their own destruction. Some of them had grown up in homes of parents who were "flower children" of the sixties. These girls were suffering the consequences of their parents' sins. It is likely that if those girls have children, many of those children will suffer the consequences of their mothers' sins also. No one can guess how many generations will be affected by the sins of the generation of the sixties.

Sin always has consequences, even if the sinner has repented, and often children are the ones most lastingly affected. There are also children in affluent homes in which parents have no interest in God. Those children are just as deprived as the others are. Lack of moral guidance will definitely affect how those children choose to live their lives. It will also lessen the likelihood that the child will ever know God.

THE GENERAL RULE

Most of us have known parents who were faithful to God and tried to train their children in the way that they should go, but still lost a child to Satan. Those parents likely prayed as diligently for their children as others prayed, but it was all to no avail. Such parents usually feel a sense of failure, frustration and, yes, injustice!

The passage that plagues their sleepless nights is Proverbs 22:6: *"Train up a child in the way that he should go, and when he is old, he will not turn from it."* It is that "general rule" principle again. While it is more likely that a child who is trained in the ways of the Lord will continue in that direction, there are exceptions.

The Lord Himself described such a scenario in Ezekiel 18, the passage previously mentioned. Ultimately, no matter how the child is trained, it is that child who will choose whether to follow God or to carry the flames of destruction. Once, we were all children. As we grew to adulthood, we got to choose the kind of person we would be. We all had varying degrees of influence from parents, aunts, uncles, grandparents, neighbors, friends, etc. In the final analysis, the decision was ours.

One very interesting passage on this subject is found in Psalm 58:3: *"Even from birth the wicked go astray. From the womb, they are wayward and speak lies."* Perhaps you have known a family in which one child seemed rebellious from infancy. The parents might have tried every approach in an effort to redirect that child's nature, but they were unsuccessful. Hopefully, such cases are rare.

It is much more common that unrighteous parents can successfully propagate a heritage of sinful children. We see it happen repeatedly as we study the Old Testament. King Ahab and other wicked kings of Israel propagated a progeny of unrighteousness.

The general rule is that righteous parents will teach their offspring the ways of the Lord, and they will grow up to follow His ways. God told the Israelites (parents), *"Teach them (God's laws) to your children, talking about them when you sit at home and when you walk along the road, when you lie down and when you get up"* (Deuteronomy 11:19).

Since this was the Lord's formula for rearing godly children, would we not be wise to incorporate it into our way of parenting?

One modern expert said that if a parent could instill honesty and a spirit of charity in the child, that child would become a good adult. However, teaching our children daily about God and His Word would give them those two traits—plus many more qualities that should make them a godly adult. Such teaching is more likely to produce greener twigs that won't burn quite so easily when the raging fire draws near.

> *"Teach them to your children, talking about them when you sit at home and when you walk along the road, when you lie down and when you get up."*
> —Deuteronomy 11:19

There are several parent/child relationships in Scripture which provoke our thinking and cause us to wonder exactly what went awry. Many of the most prominent names in the Bible produced ungodly offspring—starting with Adam and Eve. Their son, Cain, actually murdered his brother. Rebekah and Isaac produced Esau, who married into the heathen community and produced an ungodly nation. Jacob's sons became the original "twelve tribes of Israel," and yet they contemplated murdering their brother, Joseph. The sons of the priest, Eli, were vile and wicked, as were the sons of the prophet Samuel. Of course, David's sons were unthinkably wicked. Some of David's sons committed fratricide, while Absalom wanted to destroy his father.

Were these Old Testament parents inept in their parenting skills? Did they forget to talk about the word of the Lord as they walked along the road or as they sat at home? If we scrutinize the scriptural account of their lives, we have no problem pinpointing certain flaws in these parents. However, if any of us were put under such a microscope, might we also be shown to be less than perfect—no matter how exemplary we may have thought our parenting to be?

Actually, the Lord never makes reference to their failures to set the right example. In First Kings 9:4, He said to Solomon, *"If you walk before me in integrity of heart and uprightness, as David your father did…"* Although we know that at times David failed to set a good example, his life is commended by the Lord as an example to be followed. His life was exemplary because he faithfully—not perfectly—followed the Lord.

These biblical parents were rebuked primarily for failing to restrain the wrongdoing of their children. In I Samuel 3:13, it is said, *"For I told him that I would judge his family forever because of the sin he knew*

> *If today's parents wish to take a lesson from God's view of parenting, it might be: Do not fail to restrain and discipline your children.*

about; his sons made themselves contemptible, and he failed to restrain them." If today's parents wish to take a lesson from God's view of parenting, it might be: Do not fail to restrain and discipline your children.

WHAT MAKES US WHO WE ARE

When it comes to analyzing why people choose to follow the Lord or be swept away with the burning underbrush, we should factor in the numerous influences that surround us. What really makes a person who he is?

1.   Our genetic makeup obviously plays a role, and Scripture seems to agree. Earlier, we quoted Psalm 58:3, *"Even from birth...."* No one understands the exact degree to which genetic predisposition affects the outcome of who we are.

2.   The home environment can possibly overcome some of our perverse genetic traits. That is the tool being recommended in Deuteronomy 11, *"Talk about them...when you sit at home."* The home environment is no doubt a powerful influence, and some think it is the most influential. Most of us had different shades of training in the homes in which we were reared. Some parents carefully taught us to love the Lord; others did not. Some parents were believers; others were not. In some cases, one parent was a faithful believer, and the other parent was not. There are so many scenarios for the home environment. Some children grew up in institutional care, without the benefit of parents. Even so, the quality of that care would be a major factor in the person's life. The home is a major factor in molding our character.

3.   Society or our general culture will play a significant role in forming our character and personality. This
would include our peers in school and in church, our
neighbors and teachers throughout life. It also includes
television, movies, newspapers, magazines and the
Internet. These cultural factors tend to be part of the raging fire, contributing to the moral decline in our country
today. There are countless children growing up, being
molded by what they experience in our culture.

4.   Several other factors will contribute to the person
that we become. These would be such things as the quality of our health, our physical appearance and even our
intelligence. Our culture places great value on such things
as physical beauty and athletic ability, and those factors
will affect how we think about ourselves, how we are
treated and how we treat other people.

All of these things, and perhaps others, will affect who
we are and who our children will be. Nevertheless, God
has spoken. Each of us is responsible and accountable for
whether we choose to follow God or go astray.

BUT I PRAYED FOR MY CHILD

Yet, when our own precious children go astray, we
want God to intervene. We pray that He will somehow
bring the wanderer back to the fold. This is that precious
lost sheep of the parable, which we read in Luke 15. No
one cares more than God does when our children go
astray, and no one is able to do more to cause that dear
one to come back.

Teaching by parable in Matthew 18:12, Jesus said:

What do you think? If a man owns a hundred sheep, and one of them wanders away, will he not leave the ninety-nine on the hills and go to look for the one that wandered off? And if he finds it, I tell you the truth, he is happier about that one sheep than about the ninety-nine that did not wander off. In the same way, your Father in heaven is not willing that any of these little ones should be lost!

Can we think for one moment that God cares less than we do about our children who go astray? Our heavenly Father has many that have wandered away, and He knows, even better than we do, in what great jeopardy they live. Each one is precious to Him.

> *God has many tools at His disposal to retrieve these lost ones.*

God has many tools at His disposal to retrieve these lost ones. One of the greatest tools is the staying power of His Word. If our children were taught God's Word in their younger years, some of it will still be there in the recesses of their hearts. Some of the training that you gave them is still a part of who they are. One of my children told me during those vulnerable teenage years, "I can't enjoy doing anything wrong, for feeling guilty." God's Word is powerful!

One man told me that his grandmother had taught him about the Lord when he was a child, and she urged him to be a preacher when he grew up. But during his teenage years, he chose the wrong friends, and he became an alcoholic. That raging fire consumed him. His life became a disaster, and he eventually lived on the streets. However, there came a day when he remembered what his grand-mother had taught him. He decided to get help for his alcoholism, and he returned to the Lord. Today, he preaches God's Word.

There is another effective tool used by God—it is peo-ple! God may be able to put some special person into the life of your wayward child. It might be just the person who can influence that child to abandon his lost condi-tion. I personally try to stay alert to young people who might just decide to "try church" again. They are some-one's lost children. They will say something like, "I haven't been to church much lately." Each one of us should make it our ministry to watch for those precious lost sheep.

No one can know all the tools that God has at His dis-posal, but He said that He has another one! It is called adversity. This is the one that brought the prodigal home in the parable of the lost son in Luke 15. This young man had gone against everything that he had ever been taught. He squandered his money in wild living. After a while, he began to reap the consequences of his sinful life. He was suffering pain and misery. That suffering caused him to *come to his senses.* He was genuinely sorry and decided to go home and hoped that his father would let him be a hired hand.

In that parable, the father was overjoyed that his son had at last come home. We do not know how many years that father had waited and watched for him to come back. We do know that he had been watching, because the passage said, "*While he was still a long way off, his father saw him.*" That father had never lost hope. There is probably no human anywhere whose soul is totally incapable of being reached, given the right conditions. So, to any parent who has a lost child, never give up but keep watching and praying!

WHEN GOD SEEMS UNFAIR

"I consider that our present sufferings are not worth comparing with the glory that will be revealed in us."

Romans 8:18

After becoming king over Israel, David reigned in Hebron for seven years. Then the king and his men marched to Jerusalem and conquered the Jebusites. David then took up residence in the fortress and called it "the city of David." He became increasingly powerful, because the Lord was with him.

Fresh from soundly defeating the Philistines, David began making preparations to move the ark of God from Baalah of Judah to Jerusalem. The reign of David had been going very well, and the Lord had blessed his every effort. II Samuel 6:3 said, "*They set the ark of God on a new cart...*"—which was not according to the instructions given to Moses. Then the passage said:

"*...Uzzah reached out and took hold of the ark of God, because the oxen stumbled. The anger of the Lord burned against Uzzah because of his irreverent act; therefore God struck him down, and he died there beside the ark of God. Then David was angry because the Lord's wrath had broken out against Uzzah...*"

Man sometimes disagrees with the Lord's divine decrees. Man even becomes angry and feels abandoned. Those emotions seemed to be David's response God's action against Uzzah. David refused to take the ark to Jerusalem—perhaps that ark wasn't a safe item to have as part of their religion. He even seemed to fear that God might no longer be looking after his best interest.

As we face a time of spiritual decline taking hold in our land, we may feel as if we are losing ground. We wonder if we are still finding favor in God's eyes. We wonder if He is still on our side. The raging fire is gaining momentum. It is loud—almost deafening in its aggression against Christianity. We need to get our minds really clear about who God is and how He relates to injustices and calamities that may happen to us. When we start judging God—where He should have been and what He should have done—we are on thin ice. We must remember that it is God who is omniscient—not us!

> *The fact that the fire is there doesn't mean that God isn't.*

Scriptures tell us in Proverbs 3:5, *"Lean not on your own understanding,"* but we are so prone to do it. We are attempting to lean on our own understanding when life hands us a setback, and we ask, "Why?" We have difficulty believing that God's ways really are higher than our ways. We think that we can figure out the whole complex matter! The fact that the fire is there doesn't mean that God isn't.

Helen Keller's teacher, Annie Sullivan, once said to Helen, "There is one who watches over you. Do you know anything about God?" From her dark world Helen replied, "Oh yes! I've known Him a long time. I just didn't know what to call Him. He is all that has kept me from complete despair."

Helen Keller had perceived that God had played some role in her life. He had supplied some indefinable source of comfort, even though He did not restore her eyesight.

We tend to think that it is God's role to make sure that the brush fires don't get out of control. We have certain expectations for what we think God should be doing for us. He should keep us from getting burned by the fire. He should keep away the rain if we are having an outdoor event; bring rain if our yards need water; keep us out of danger; help us find a parking place; keep us from ill health, etc.

In general, this begins to sound as if He is supposed to be our Magic Genie who takes care of our every need or desire. If that is our only perception of God, we are probably in for some serious faith struggles. Helen Keller found comfort from knowing a presence of God—even in her dark world. He had not taken away her problems.

It will not be the successes, gifts, and goodies that make our walk with God stable and secure. It will be when we finally grasp that He is all-powerful and in control of everything. Everything! Only then will we have a perspective that will allow us to sense God's presence, even when our personal world is dark. Only then can we have a faith that strengthens us when we must stand strong against the raging fire—a faith that will help us to have the wisdom never to turn against God.

The Lord spoke through Isaiah and said, *"For as the heavens are higher than the earth, so are my ways higher than your ways and my thoughts than your thoughts"* (Isaiah 55:9). The vastness between heaven and earth is not even comprehensible to us.

> *It will not be the successes, gifts, and goodies that make our walk with God stable and secure.*

Yet, people continue to base their faith on how many trinkets God will toss their way. There is some tendency to think that if good things are happening, God must be very pleased with us. Then, when things start going wrong, we are hurt and blame God.

There was an airplane crash a few years ago in Dallas, and although it was a horrific crash, there were very few fatalities. Soon, there was a story in the newspaper about a man who said that he now believes in God. Why? Because that crash had been so bad, and yet so few had died.

While it was wonderful to think that man had come to believe in God, there was something troublesome about what had caused him to believe. If the basis of his faith was that everything turned out right, what will happen to his faith when things go wrong?

A SENSE OF INJUSTICE

For most people there is probably a little more substance to their faith. Even so, when life causes us pain, we are somewhat inclined to question God. In fact, it may be the really faithful who feel the greatest sense of injustice.

In Job 21, Job spoke, feeling a deep sense of injustice that although he had been faithful to God, he was suffering intense physical pain as well as the emotional loss of all his children and his wealth. Meanwhile, he saw others who cared nothing for God, and they were prospering. They had nice homes. They had children and grandchildren. They were free from fear—having good times and lots of fun. But out of their prosperity, those wicked people were not crediting God. They seemed to think that they had brought about this prosperity for themselves, and they said, *"Leave us alone. We have no desire to know your ways. Who is the Almighty that we should serve him? What would we gain by praying to him?"*

> *Prosperity can be a greater test of character than adversity.*

Those people had been given enough comfort and ease to allow themselves the luxury of turning their focus inward to feel self-importance and self-will. And the will of God has always run counter to such an attitude. Their trinkets, prizes, and successes had not caused them to trust God. In fact, their worldly treasures had driven them away from God!

Historically, it has been in a time of prosperity and peace that Satan can most easily take man by the hand and lead him away from God. It has been when man had the leisure and luxury to take his ego on a stroll about the options of life. He could always conjure many ideas about how to make himself happier—without God!

Prosperity can be a greater test of character than adversity. Man can decide that he is very wise—otherwise how could he be living in such "good times?" Perhaps he does not need God after all! When things go seem to go well without praying to God, man may give God no credit!

That very behavior is reflected in the history of the Hebrew people of the Old Testament as they repeatedly forgot their God. Things would go well for them for a while, then they would become evil and turn away from

God. Then disaster would strike them, and they would wonder why their God was not there looking after them. They could never understand what had happened.

GOD CAN GET OUR ATTENTION

The writer of Judges 6:1 said, "*Again the Israelites did evil in the eyes of the Lord, and for seven years He gave them into the hands of the Midianites.*" Those Midianites terrorized them and destroyed their crops and cattle. The passage said, "*The Midianites so impoverished the Israelites that they cried out to the Lord for help.*"

In response to their pleas for help, the angel of the Lord came to a young man named Gideon and said, "*The Lord is with you.*"

Now, note Gideon's reply, "*But sir, if the Lord is with us, why has all this happened to us? The Lord has abandoned us and put us into the hand of Midian.*" Gideon did not even understand who had moved. Drifting away from God is often done with such subtlety.

Man often does not seek God's assistance until the raging fire threatens to consume him.

Sometimes, he calls upon God only as a last resort. The attitudes of men in the modern world reflect the ways of those ancient Israelites. We may experience times when the grass is green and the skies are blue, so we may forget to nurture our relationship with God. It may not be outright denial

It may not be outright denial of God, but we don't allow His opinions to count for much!

of God, but we don't allow His opinions to count for much. We may let our prayer life grow stagnant—our dependence on Him may wane. We don't read His Word regularly and don't make our choices based upon the will of God.

The people of this country have become quite similar to the Israelites of the Old Testament. This country was founded upon strong religious principles, based upon the teachings of God. But the vast populace across the land today rarely mentions God or His will for us. Like those people of whom Job spoke—the ones who felt that they had nothing to gain by serving God, they want nothing to do with God. It would only interfere with their good times. Today, people might say,

> *Man can easily decide that God's principles were meant for another time and place.*

"After all, God is out of step with our times. A God that says things like, 'Men should be the head of the household as Christ is head of the church' is politically incorrect. A God that says, 'Homosexuality is detestable' in an age when everything is supposed to be acceptable is intolerant. A God that calls things 'absolutely wrong and sinful' doesn't belong in an age when right and wrong are a matter of personal opinion." Man can easily decide that God's principles were meant for another time and place.

Then come the Midianites—bankruptcy, crime, moral decay, terminal illness or death of someone near and dear, the family collapses, and children become criminals.

Then, man starts judging God and wondering where He is in all of this. What kind of God would let this happen?

Like Gideon, people say, "If we are God's people, why are bad things happening? He used to be with us—but He left."

BARGAINING WITH GOD

It is interesting to observe that even those who have not thought of God in years somehow expect Him to show up when there is trouble. They often bargain with God—"If you will let this illness turn out not to be terminal, I will actually start going to church." Man never tires of trying to manipulate God as if He were an over-indulgent, permissive parent. Even Abraham tried to bargain when he really wanted something from God. He wanted his nephew, Lot, spared when God planned to destroy Sodom. So Abraham asked, "If there are fifty righteous people in Sodom, will you spare the city? (No way will there be fifty.) How about thirty? Ten?"

Jacob, likewise, bargained with God when in deep trouble: "If you will get me through this, I will be your person." And today, mankind bargains with God when he desperately needs something. It must be amusing to God that man thinks himself so powerful that he can make his own deal with the Creator of all things.

Even when we have remained close to God and faithful in our walk with Him, the fall-out from Satan's raging fire may put our faith to the test and cause us to wonder if God is really there. In the midst of our polluted and perverted culture, it is difficult for us to remember that God knows how to work all things to His purpose. It is too complex for us. Isaiah said, "And His understanding no one can fathom." (Isaiah 40:28)

SHOULD THE FAITHFUL BE SPARED?

It is quite possible that even the righteous may suffer some of the consequences of this spiritual decline. In a number of places in Scripture, God made it abundantly clear that the righteous will not be spared the adversities of life. In Matthew 5:45, the writer said that God *"causes His sun to rise on the evil and the good."* He also said that rain is sent upon the righteous and the unrighteous alike. When the fire is really raging, both the straight green trees and the dry stubble are vulnerable. If the rain comes to quench the fire, both the stubble and the green trees will benefit. And the Living Water is available to both the godly and the ungodly.

As we read the New Testament, we see that the apostles certainly were not spared, and the Christians of the New Testament church were not spared from the problems created by the culture of their time. Of course, Christ Himself was not spared. Much of what Peter wrote in the New Testament was written to Christians, urging them to bear up under the pain of persecution.

Still, when we have a close relationship with God, it is difficult for us to avoid thinking that because of that relationship we deserve special consideration in return for our meritorious faithfulness. We may not quite have the nerve to speak it in just those words, but deep down in our heart of hearts, we are thinking that perhaps God owes us something.

Then, one day, the bottom drops out of our lives—we are scorched by Satan's fire, and we decide that God is unfair. We raise a bloody fist and shake it in anger at God. "If this is what you do to your friends, what do you do to your enemies? If my best human friend did this to me, our friendship would be over." God gets the blame and Satan smiles

> *. . . deep down in our heart of hearts, we are thinking that perhaps God owes us something.*

his cynical smile of satisfaction, because he is seeing a Christian tottering on the brink of turning away from God.

When Job looked and saw the wicked prospering, he could not have been privileged to know some of the things that we are blessed to know through God's written Word. We have access to Scriptures, which tell us that we can anticipate eternal life. Even with that information, something tends to fog our brains when the sparks are flying over our heads, and we forget what God has told us. So, we tend to respond to God as if He had never told us to expect trouble.

We engage in an unproductive exercise when we decide that it is unfair of God to allow those who are a part of the raging fire to prosper. It is a wasteful use of our emotions to look at someone who is not living right and judge that they deserve this adversity more than we do.

WHAT WOULD IT TAKE?

Job did some of that very human kind of thinking as he sat scratching his sores with broken pieces of pottery, having lost everything. Most of us have not lost everything. If we were to lose everything, would that cause us to turn away from God? Satan obviously thinks it is a possibility, based on his conversation with God in the first chapter of Job. In Job 1:11, Satan said, *"But stretch out your hand and strike everything he has, and he will surely curse you to your face."*

Satan took all Job's possessions. Would that cause us to leave God? For some, it would! We are very fond of our possessions. Some would leave the church and reproach God.

Satan took Job's precious children for whom he had been so careful to pray. Would that do it? For some, it would! They would say, "Any God who would let this happen is not the God I worship."

Satan took Job's health and ravaged his body with pain and ugly sores. Would that do it? For some, it would! They would say, "If all this can befall me, there is no God."

Job did not leave God although he did want to debate the issue with Him. His belief in God would not waver, and he said, *"Though He slay me, yet will I hope in Him."* Even though Job had lost so much, he had not lost his faith.

What would we do if we encountered adversity similar to that of Job? What if Satan's raging fire were to take away everything? Would we accomplish anything, if in bitterness and anger we turned away from God because of adversity in our lives? "We'll show Him! We won't be on His side anymore!" (It would be like a gerbil confronting a lion.) In fact, When God finally responded to Job's anger, He showed Job that only God is in control (Job 38-41).

ANALYZING OUR ANGER

> *Anger camouflages the real problem and makes it more difficult to resolve the issue.*

It has been said that anger is actually a secondary response, which is triggered by some other primary emotion. Anger camouflages the real problem and makes it more difficult to resolve the issue. In other words, anger is only an offshoot of some other emotion. So, the next time we find ourselves dealing with anger toward God, we might ask which of the following primary emotions could possibly be the real culprit:

1.   A feeling of rejection or abandonment is a primary emotion. This is common with a child whose parent has left the family for a romantic fling. Or, sometimes we feel abandoned when some evil befalls us, and we think that we should have been protected. We see this in children who have been abused and sense that at least one of the parents should have given protection. The primary feeling or emotion is rejection or abandonment. The secondary response is anger, so there is an angry young person.

It is the same response that a believer in God may have. Job felt abandonment by a God to whom he had been faithful. His sense of rejection produced anger.

2.   A feeling of injustice is a primary emotion. It is a sense that things have not been done in a fair and equitable manner. A man may have worked loyally for a company for twenty years, and some rookie gets the promotion. Job had served the Lord diligently, and he lost his children, his property, and his health. He looked around and saw unfaithful people prospering and enjoying a good life. He felt a strong sense of injustice. The feeling of injustice is what brought about that secondary response of anger.

3.   Fear and insecurity are primary emotions. A man may die, leaving a wife with young children to rear. In addition, she may have to try to financially support those children. We can only imagine the fear and insecurity that she might experience. Anger is an offshoot of that initial fear. In our Grief Recovery program, it is pointed out that the surviving spouse may actually feel anger toward the spouse who has died because she is left with responsibilities that she feels incapable of handling.

4.   Frustration is a primary emotion. It is felt when experiencing a problem over which we have no control. Infertility is typical of a situation in which a person desperately desires something but does not have the ability to fix the problem. The resulting emotion is frustration. In the Old Testament, Rachel, unable to have children, wailed, "Give me children, or I die!" The ultimate response to frustration may be anger.

Anger's root cause comes from a violation of perceived rights. For a believer, resolving anger against God can best be accomplished when we genuinely accept that God is sovereign. This is exactly what God was teaching as He finally responded to Job in those final chapters of the book of Job. That is why the reading of the book of Job is so helpful. It teaches us so much about avoiding the pitfalls that might ensnare us when we must endure hardship and adversity.

There was recently a newspaper story that captured the sad futility of turning away from God in anger. It was a story about Dr. Elizabeth Kubler-Ross. She is a Swiss-born psychiatrist who became famous for her studies about death and dying—and the stages of grief. She married an American doctor and moved to Chicago. Her book entitled "On Death and Dying" was published in 1969 and revolutionized the way Americans look at that subject. In fact, it launched the Hospice program in the United States.

She had believed in God and in life after death. She had always encouraged patients to believe in "a good God who would help them." Along the way, she became involved with New Age spiritualists and came to believe that there is no death—that one is just reincarnated. Her involvement with channeling and spirits took its toll at home. In 1976, her husband gave himself a Father's Day present—he divorced her.

Today, incapacitated by a series of strokes, Dr. Elizabeth Kubler-Ross sits in the corner of her home in the desert of

Arizona, smoking cigarettes, watching television, waiting to die and cursing God.

"My only regret," she says, "is that for forty years I spoke of a good God who helps people. Well, that's baloney. Don't believe a word of it."

Her conversation is filled with complaining. She is angry about her care when in the hospital. She is furious that she must sit in a chair and depend upon someone else to make her a cup of tea. And her voice is tinged with bitterness.

If asked in which of the five stages of grief she finds herself at the moment, she disdainfully yells, "Anger! Yes, I am mad!"

She has left God. She is alone without God. To purposely turn out the Light of the World must leave one in terrible darkness.

We cannot understand what is going on when the ways of the world seem to be winning. God obviously knows that in our human form we cannot fathom an explanation. That is why He did not bother explaining anything to Job. He just said "Trust me." God has always called upon His people to trust Him with their adversity. Our task is not to judge God, but to stay faithful to Him.

It has been said, "If we stay faithful to God, the only hell we will ever know is right here on earth. If we turn away from Him, the only Heaven we will ever know is right here on earth."

RELATIONSHIPS TESTED BY SIN

"Woe to those who call evil good and good evil, who put darkness for light and light for darkness, who put bitter for sweet and sweet for bitter."

Isaiah 5:20

A few years ago in Phoenix, Arizona, a family Christmas tree erupted in flames as the mother lay sleeping on the sofa. Her six-year-old son awakened her and then ran to the back of the house. She apparently tried to put out the fire herself, but Christmas trees virtually explode when they catch fire. The smoke quickly overcame her. The six-year-old found his sister in the back bedroom and tried to get her to run outside with him, but she refused to go. Finally, the boy released his sister's hand and ran outside. By the time firefighters and police arrived, the house was engulfed in flames. The boy told them that his mother and sister were still inside the house. As firefighters entered, wearing their protective gear, they disappeared through black billowing smoke. Soon one of the men emerged, carrying the body of the mother, who had tried to fight a fire for which she was not equipped. Then the second firefighter returned carrying the body of the sister, who had not wanted to leave the burning house. Saving people from an inferno is a risky and uncertain business—especially when they don't want to be rescued.

> *Sometimes it takes desperate measures in order to salvage a soul.*

When friends or family members are caught in swirling flames of sin, those closest to them feel ill equipped to rescue them. Sometimes it takes desperate measures in order to salvage a soul. It always takes many hours of prayer, heartbreak, and tears. Our relationship with that person will become strained and may actually be broken. We tend to take the responsibility upon ourselves to set that person's life back in order. But like that mother fighting the flames of the Christmas tree, we are not equipped. We can encourage and support, but the person in that flaming whirlwind of sin will have to decide to leave it.

> *We live in a world that tells us, "Do whatever makes you happy."*

We live in a world that tells us, "Do whatever makes you happy" or "It's right if you say it's right." That attitude has fanned the flames of immorality in our country. With so much social pollution, we can expect a certain amount of contamination in the church and in our physical families. More and more frequently we find ourselves faced with a complex question: How am I supposed to respond when a friend or a family member is engaged in some deadly sin?

Most of us would go to battle with Satan in order to reclaim that lost soul if possible. But like the young girl in the Christmas tree fire in Phoenix, the lost soul may not wish to be rescued. It can be a very difficult struggle when the lost friend or family member doesn't want help.

Furthermore, there will be those who think that we have no right to confront the sin of other people. Almost immediately someone will say, "Let him who is without sin cast the first stone." That point does strike a nerve, for after all, they are the words of Jesus, and none of us is sinless. So, are we supposed to say nothing and act as if such outrageous misconduct is acceptable?

Our culture has adopted the idea that tolerance and acceptance should be the stars in our crowns. Therefore, we commonly hear statements like, "We all need forgiveness at times." Who can deny that? But does it mean that there are no boundaries? If so, we may as well close the courthouse and open the prison doors. After all, every one of us needs forgiveness.

Today, there seems to be something archaic or old-fashioned about referring to sin as "sin." In fact people tend to scoff and smirk when the word "sin" is used, and we run the risk of being called Pharisaical. The prayer of the Pharisee in Luke 18 has always been used to attack self-righteousness—and rightly so! But it has also been used as a tool of Satan to restrain any effort to identify and reprove sin. Another passage often quoted is Matthew 7:1, *"Do not judge, or you too will be judged. For in the same way you judge others, you will be judged, and with the measure you use, it will be measured to you."* This passage is also a favorite used to deny a Christian's ability or responsibility to reprove sin.

Yet, in Luke 17, the writer said, *"If your brother sins, rebuke him, and if he repents, forgive him."* Many other passages also charge Christians with the responsibility of recognizing sin. The writer of Matthew 18 even gave specific steps for dissolving the relationship when a brother refuses to repent. Such action requires judgment. Obviously, God does want sin identified and rebuked— especially in a brother.

It is essential that we clearly understand our charge in regard to reproving sin. Otherwise, we will find ourselves following the world into the politically correct mindset of live and let live, or more accurately, "sin and let sin." We may be dangerously close to that attitude already. Such a view is devoid of principle and denies God's authority. If sin is not condemned, it is only a matter of time before it is accepted.

A LIFESTYLE OR A SIN?

It is unlikely that any of us has escaped having our lives touched by at least one of today's prevalent social sins. These godless excesses catch us off balance, because the change in values has come about so quickly in our society.

There was a time when we hardly knew what a homosexual really was. At one time, many states had a law against sodomy. It was a crime! But almost overnight, we find ourselves being asked to believe that homosexual behavior is an acceptable way of life. Some corporations are now offering family benefits to homosexual partners, even though most states have not legalized their marriages. With the help of the media and Hollywood, homosexuals are lobbying powerfully for certain legislated rights—especially employment rights. They want the right to teach our children and to work in programs such as Boy Scouts. One look at some of their "Gay Pride" parades would horrify any concerned parent.

There is no question that Scripture calls such behavior detestable before God. In Romans 1:26, 27, Paul wrote about God's wrath against mankind, and he said:

Because of this, God gave them over to shameful lusts. Even their women exchanged natural relations for unnatural ones. In the same way the men also abandoned natural relations with women and were inflamed with lust for one another. Men committed indecent acts with other men, and received in themselves the due penalty for their perversion.

The inspired Word of God clearly considers homosexuality an unacceptable lifestyle. It was condemned in Scripture consistently. The pagans used male prostitutes in their temples, and the practice was called detestable (I Kings 14:24).

The sin of homosexuality is certainly not a new sin. It was the sin most prevalent in Sodom. It would appear that the vast majority of men and boys in that ancient city had become homosexuals. Genesis 19:4 said, "...*all the men from every part of the city of Sodom—both young and old—surrounded the house.*" The men of Sodom had become so depraved they insisted that the two men, who were angels, be brought out so that they could "*have sex with them.*"

Did God view homosexuality as an acceptable lifestyle? Genesis 19:24 said, "*Then the Lord rained down burning sulfur on Sodom and Gomorrah—from the Lord out of the heavens. Thus he overthrew those cities and the entire plain, including all those living in the cities—and also the vegetation in the land.*" It would appear that the Lord was angry and had no intention of giving them "acceptable lifestyle" status.

In the New Testament, Peter referred back to the destruction of Sodom, and his words have serious implications for our world today. In II Peter 2:6, he said, "...*he* (God) *condemned the cities of Sodom and Gomorrah by burning them to ashes and made them an example of what is going to happen to the ungodly.*" Someone recently said that Hell would not necessarily be a place of fire but a place where God is absent. Clearly, God will

> *That cataclysmic time at Sodom was meant to get our attention.*

not be there, but this passage and others sound as if fire will be there! That cataclysmic time at Sodom was meant to get our attention.

WHEN THE OFFENDER IS FAMILY

Nevertheless, families who are faithful Christians have faced the heartbreak of losing their children, both boys and girls, to the homosexual community. Some of their children have openly told the parents that they are living with a homosexual partner. The dilemma for those parents will be that of relationship. How should this matter be handled?

When parents read the story of the prodigal son in Luke 15, they see a father who never lost hope that his son would return. Of course, the father of the prodigal had no decision to make about whether to maintain a relationship while his son lived in sin. His son was gone to some distant place. Conversely, today's parents may have a child living in the perverse sin of homosexuality right in his own city. Those parents have a decision to make.

Among families interviewed, one decided to accept their son even though he made the sin of homosexuality his ongoing way of life. They have also allowed his partner to come to their home. They do not approve, but they make no demands.

Another family decided to maintain a relationship with their son, but they never allow the partner to come to their home. They hope that by "leaving the door open," they may encourage their son to come out of his sinful life.

All of these parents felt that they must make it clear that they believe homosexuality to be a sin and that they do not approve of it. It is the question of relationship that creates a serious dilemma for them. Sin strains and fractures relationships.

> *Relationships stabilize and normalize life for all of us.*

The church tends to practice "don't ask, don't tell," although the majority of practicing homosexual prodigals have left the church. Some of them attend a nondenominational church for homosexuals. These have no intention of leaving that sinful way of life, but they would like to keep their relationship with friends and family.

Relationships stabilize and normalize life for all of us. Loss of relationships brings loneliness and disrupts one's sense of well being. It is in the area of relationship that sin plunges its dagger and twists it. Neither the sinner nor those who love him escape the pain.

IT'S MY FRIEND! WHAT DO I DO?

It is becoming more common to learn that one of our longtime friends is a part of the homosexual community. We are shocked and sad, but what are we supposed to do? Do we continue the friendship and pretend not to know? It is not usually possible today, because the homosexual frequently confesses and tries to persuade us that his choice of lifestyle should be accepted.

Recently, a young man received an e-mail from a good friend that he had known in college. The friend just wanted to be candid with him and let him know that he is now homosexual. The friend further stated that he hoped that their friendship would continue as usual.

Upon receiving the e-mail, the young man responded by saying that he would like to recommend counseling for his friend, because he considered homosexuality a sin. He said, "I could no more have a close friendship with you than with an adulterer." He added that he would be pleased to support and encourage him if he chose to try to leave that sinful way of life.

Relationships are regularly being confronted with this question. Because this matter is so prevalent, we need to know what the Word of God admonished us to do. In the continuation of Paul's treatise on perverted sexual behavior, in Romans 1:32 he said, "*Although they know God's righteous decree that those who do such things deserve death, they not only continue to do those very things, but also approve of those who practice them."* According to this passage and others, we must make certain that our disapproval is known. Then, in Ephesians 5:11, Paul spelled it out clearly, *"Have nothing to do with the fruitless deeds of darkness but rather expose them."*

In the Old Testament, the Lord opposed alliances with people who did wicked things. In II Chronicles 18 and 19, a spectacular illustration was given through Jehoshaphat, King of Judah. Although he had been a king who respected God, he moved ever closer in his relationship with the evil King Ahab. He finally decided to form a liaison with Ahab to go to war against Ramoth Gilead. He said to Ahab, *"I am as you are and my people as your people. We will join you in war."* There was, of course, a certain kinship between these people, but there was a vast chasm that separated them in respect to their faithfulness to God.

> *"Have nothing to do with the fruitless deeds of darkness but rather expose them."*
> —*Ephesians 5:11*

Before going into battle, Jehoshaphat wanted to inquire of God, so Ahab brought four hundred of his prophets. They promptly prophesied what they knew the wicked Ahab wanted to hear—"Go to battle!"

But Jehoshaphat asked if there were a prophet who could inquire directly of the Lord. *"Well,"* said Ahab, *"there is one named Micaiah but I never use him, because he never prophesies anything good about me."* They sent for Micaiah and he prophesied that Ahab would die if they went to war with Ramoth Gilead. Ahab promptly had him thrown into prison.

The two kings led their armies into battle, and just as Micaiah had prophesied, Ahab was killed. As King Jehoshaphat was returning to Judah, the prophet Jehu went out to meet him and brought a message from the Lord, "*Should you help the wicked and love those who hate the Lord? Because of this, the wrath of the Lord is upon you.*"

> *Relationship is one of the tools that the Lord employs in order to coax the sinner back into the fold.*

Relationship is one of the tools that the Lord employs in order to coax the sinner back into the fold. If our friends freely choose a way of life that dishonors God, they should not be in our circle of friends. They cannot enjoy the benefits and security of their former relationships. We should always make it clear that we still love them and miss their friendship, but their soul is more important. We will constantly pray for an end to their rebellion against the teachings of God.

Once a person has participated in the homosexual way of life, it is said to be very difficult to leave that sin. Some Bible scholars believe that loss of ability to have natural relations with the opposite sex is the meaning of the passage in Romans 1:27, which states, *Men committed indecent acts with other men, and received in themselves the due penalty for their perversion.*" There are organizations that have helped people in that effort, and today there are those who believe that they have freed themselves from their slavery to the condition. It may require more effort than some people are willing to expend. Like many other sins, the battle may be a long and uncertain struggle, but freedom will be worth the effort. There are former homosexuals in the church today, living a celibate life. They seem very joyful in their new life, and we praise God for their transformed lives.

SIN STRAINS RELATIONSHIPS

Relationships will always be a barometer of how things are going when there is a raging fire of moral decay and spiritual decline. When sin invades, relationships will almost immediately begin to feel the strain. If there is a friend or family member in the clutches of alcohol, adultery, drugs, or pornography, they usually begin to distance themselves from those closest to them. These sinful addictions can happen at any age and at any socioeconomic level. It may be a wife, a mother, a husband, a father, a teenager, or other relative.

A recent survey has found that one out of four children live with an alcoholic today. It is a stressful, chaotic environment. Many children grow up in homes devastated by such sins, and it affects their lives forever. Those children may find themselves trying to be the adult in the family, struggling to assume the responsibilities that should belong to the addicted parent. That experience will always be a part of the child—even when they have grown up and married.

Families need to make serious decisions about how to cope with a family member who has become a victim to the lure of alcohol, drugs and adultery. But often they make the decision to make no decision. Usually, families are longsuffering—sometimes to the detriment of the other family members. Family members tend to "cover" for the alcoholic or addict. Sometimes, parents are much too slow about admitting that their child is in trouble. Family members are much too close emotionally to be able to respond objectively. Outside counseling can be very helpful. Programs such as Al-Anon are designed for family members of the alcoholic or drug dependent person.

Christians can be very supportive to families with addiction problems. Sometimes we play the role of the shepherd in steering that lost family member to the proper resource for help. Often the lost sheep wants to stay lost and refuses to return. In that case, our care and encouragement should be directed to the family, because for them, their closest relationship is in the process of disintegrating.

There are many other areas of sin that shatter relationships. Out of wedlock births have become more common in recent years. It has become so common that young women tend to keep their babies. Today, the world approves those situations and deems them quite acceptable. But once again relationships are strained, and we find ourselves wondering what should be the position of the parent or Christian friend.

Another common smoldering sin in the fabric of our society is that of people living together out of wedlock. They may eventually decide to marry, and if they do, they may decide to have an elaborate wedding. The world doesn't blink an eye, but what position should we take as Christians? On the one hand, we are pleased that they finally marry, but on the other, they degrade the institution of marriage by treating the ceremony as if it were only an optional formality.

Once again, parents are in the most awkward and painful position. They watch as their son or daughter tramples underfoot all the principles that they have taught them, but parents will go to any length to salvage the soul of their child. Surely it is not wrong to do that, but all the love and patience of that parent or family cannot spare the sinner from facing the consequences of his bad choices—usually lifelong consequences!

Whether we are a friend, relative, spouse, or parent of one who has darkened his life and reputation with sin, we care about that person. We especially care about their soul. We care about other hearts that are being influenced by what is happening. The Lord seemed to treat each sinner with customized care. We certainly are in no position to be callous or pompous when it comes to relating to other sinners.

There is a familiar story that is told of a mother's love for her wayward son. This mother's thin face was lined with sorrows that had robbed her life of its spirit. As she walked down the corridor, a set of heavy doors clanged shut behind her. She visited this prison every week. It wasn't easy, because she had to ride a bus for many miles. The bus ticket cost more than she could really afford. She dragged a chair to the screen and waited.

In the back among the cells, a scruffy young man was brought out amid shouts of profanity and taunting. It was a wretched place back there in the cellblock. He was cursed, kicked, and abused on a daily basis. The guards treated him like the lowest form of humanity. Handcuffed, his legs in chains, he shuffled into the visitation area.

"How are you, son?" she whispered. "You look so good. I miss you so much that I could hardly wait to get here today. Are they treating you well?"

"Yeah, Mom. I'm fine. You really shouldn't try to come so often."

In a matter of minutes the visit was ended. The guard came and took him back to the misery of that cellblock. He wished that she hadn't seen him the way that he was. Still, the anticipation of her visit was all that got him through the week!

The story portrays the consequences of sin as it turns lives into blackened, burned-out forests. The mother is a tragic figure, who typifies the pain brought into a relationship by sin. The son shows the importance of having someone who cares. If someone cares, there is still a ray of hope. If someone cares, there is reason to go on.

Our Creator knows that relationships sustain us and build our self-esteem. That is likely the reason He had so much to say about relationships with those who choose sin as a way of life. God loves us no less than that mother loved her son. He carefully coaxes us away from sin's grasp. He provides avenues of escape for us. In I Corinthians 10:13, Paul wrote, "*No temptation has seized* you except what is common to man. And God is faithful; he will not let you be tempted beyond what you can bear. But when you are tempted, he will provide a way out so that you can stand up under it."

> When the people that we love choose to make sin a way of life, they will suffer—and so will we!

In spite of all God's care, we sometimes allow ourselves to be drawn into the fire with all its sin and its consequences. He still loves us; He still wants us back and visits every day. But no amount of love and longsuffering will enable us to escape the *consequences* of that sin. When the people that we love choose to make sin a way of life, they will suffer—and so will we!

HOW WOULD JESUS HANDLE THIS?

The question frequently asked is "How would Jesus handle this situation?" In Scripture we see Jesus as one who was compassionate toward sinners. We should emulate His compassion and never be quick to release the hand of a sinner.

Jesus just looked at a crowd and felt compassion for their lost condition. Many of His followers had at one time lived in sin as a way of life. When they became His friends, they left that way of life. If they had not been willing to change, they would not have been His friends. The Pharisees accused Jesus of being a friend to sinners, but Jesus was changing those lives. The Pharisees felt no appreciation or joy that people were leaving sin. They were not so interested in bringing back the sinner as being sure that the sinner was kept out of their ranks. We should be the kind of "friend to sinners" that Jesus was by helping them to leave their lives of sin.

It is quite possible that we are too impatient with people at times, and we may not feel enough compassion. That is more likely to be the case when the sinner is not a member of our immediate physical family. We are usually more longsuffering with our family members.

Paul tried to teach us how to effectively restore the lost brother. For example, in Galatians 6:1 he said, *"Brothers, if someone is caught in a sin, you who are spiritual should restore him gently. But watch yourself or you may also be tempted."* A major reason that we need to be gentle and compassionate with sinners is that we ourselves are also very vulnerable to sin. We should not be proud or consider ourselves above falling into Satan's clutches.

HYPOCRISY WILL SPOIL THE PROCESS

There is an important ingredient in the process of finding and restoring a lost sheep. That ingredient is the attitude and spiritual condition of the restorer. Paul wisely inserted in Galatians 6 the qualification for persons involved in the restoration process. He said, *"You who are spiritual."* We should carefully and objectively examine our own lives to be sure that we are free of any kind of "plank" in our own eye. If there is any doubt, we should let someone else bring home the lost sheep. Any level of hypocrisy will likely destroy the genuine recovery of an erring brother.

This was exactly the problem when the "woman caught in adultery" was brought to Jesus in John 8. Her accusers were as guilty—or perhaps more so—than she was. Jesus was not dismissing her sin, for He said to her, "*Go and leave your life of sin.*" Jesus wanted to change lives and save souls; He would not have chosen to leave someone in a lost condition. In this instance, her accusers were hypocrites themselves, and Jesus never had much compassion for hypocrisy.

Any level of hypocrisy will likely destroy the genuine recovery of an erring brother.

For a sinner to be restored to the Lord, those participating in the effort must be right themselves. In Psalm 141:5, the writer said, "*Let a righteous man strike me—it is a kindness; let him rebuke me—it is oil on my head. My head will not refuse it.*"

Solomon said in Ecclesiastes 7:5, "*It is better to heed a wise man's rebuke than to listen to the song of fools.*"

There will be certain people who will be able to persuade and influence the erring heart. These are people whose genuineness and personal reputation are respected. When we are going in search of a lost sheep, we should be in prayer that God would give us the wisdom to send the right person.

DO NOT IGNORE SIN

Scripture teaches that we should never act as if nothing is amiss when there is blatant sin in our midst. Indeed, we must have compassion and perseverance, but the brother living in sin should always be confronted for the sake of his soul. Proverbs 24:24 said, "*Whoever says to the guilty 'You are innocent,' people will curse him and nations denounce him.*" In II Timothy 4:2, Paul said, "*Preach the word; be prepared in season and out of season. Correct, rebuke and encourage with great patience and careful instruction.*" These two passages as well as many others admonish us that we should never ignore obvious ongoing sin. It has a way of spawning spotty fires that spread, affecting the whole body.

Restoring the erring can be a delicate and lengthy process, requiring much love and patience. Each case is an individual matter. There is no magic formula as to the time that might be required. If the erring one refuses to cooperate, there is no alternative but to disrupt our relationship with that person.

The writer of Psalm 119:115 said, "*Away from me you evildoers.*" Paul wrote in II Thessalonians 3:6, "*Keep away from every brother who is idle and does not live according to the teachings you have received from us.*" Those instructions are sometimes painful to carry out, and many people refuse to comply with this admonition—even when elders withdraw fellowship.

Paul continued his admonition in verse II Thessalonians 3:14, "*If anyone does not obey our instructions in this letter: [1] Take note of him; [2] Do not associate with him in order that he may feel ashamed; [3] Yet, do not regard him as an enemy but warn him as a brother."*

We never should treat the erring one as an enemy. We still love this person very much; it is his sin that we hate. His sin separates him from God and from us. Christians may have mistakenly treated some of the erring ones as enemies. Our hand should always be held out to the lost with love in hope that the lost one will come back. The whole process was designed to bring the lost sheep home and restore that treasured relationship.

> *This erring one is a soul with a human body wrapped around it.*

The prophet said in Jeremiah 32:33, *"Though I taught them again and again, they would not listen or respond to discipline."* Jeremiah was persistent! Those Jews would not be persuaded because they were enslaved by sin. They believed only what they wanted to believe, and they mistreated the messenger, Jeremiah. This is a very common scenario when we try to persuade a sinner. But most of us are not so longsuffering as Jeremiah—nor are we so selfless as he was. We are often distracted by peripheral issues and forget that this erring one is a soul with a human body wrapped around it.

POWERLESS BUT POWERFUL

"My power is made perfect in weakness."
II Corinthians 12:9

As the Idaho farmer and his wife began their stroll across their farm, they could feel a brisk breeze at their backs. It was slightly cloudy, but still a nice day to take a walk across the prairie. As far as the eye could see there was beautiful yellow prairie grass.

A short time later, they found themselves trapped without a chance of outrunning a rapidly advancing prairie fire. The fire had apparently been ignited by what is known as dry lightning and was being swept by the brisk south wind. They had nothing with which to fight the fire, and they certainly were not able to stay ahead of it.

The farmer frantically reached into his pocket, and his hand emerged holding a single match. He quickly struck the match on the sole of his shoe and ignited the grass at their feet. The grass at their feet began to burn, spreading northward like the fire behind them. The man took his wife's hand and led her into the hot, blackened swath before them. They felt the heat of the scorched earth through their shoes.

The original fire at their backs crackled fiercely as it overtook them, spewing its gray smoke into their faces. Its heat parched their skin, and they choked on its smoke. But they lived!

The raging prairie fire quickly skirted the burned earth left by the farmer's life-saving fire. It left the couple standing safely on their patch of burned field. Only moments earlier, the farmer and his wife had been helpless before a racing fire that had them trapped. They were powerless against the advancing fire, but the farmer found some power in his pocket. It saved their lives.

As the raging fire of immorality and spiritual decline rushes toward us, we may feel quite powerless. Yet, like the farmer, we have a powerful resource upon which to call. We have our own fire, the Spirit living within us. We can fan that flame within and find ourselves in a secure zone.

As people of God, we shouldn't just stand around waiting to be overtaken by moral and spiritual decline. We should be living with enthusiasm, allowing God to work His purpose in our lives. His purpose can affect the course of the raging fire. We may be powerless, but with the Lord's help, we are powerful!

Powerful things happen through us when God works His purpose through our lives.

There is a familiar passage of Scripture found in Philippians 2:13, which says, *"For it is God who works in you to will and to act according to His good purpose."* Notice that the word "purpose" is singular. When Scripture speaks of God's purpose, it always seems to be singular in thrust. If God's purpose is singular in its thrust, what is that singular focus? Is it about whether my team wins or I get the best parking place?

Many years after King David's life had ended, Luke would say of him in Acts 13:36, *"For when David had served God's purpose in his own generation, he fell asleep; and he was buried with his fathers and his body decayed."* David's life had been lived for God's purpose, and the word "purpose" was singular.

Recently, Joni Erickson Tada, a quadriplegic, said, "God works in our lives in very special ways, but what He is doing has much more to do with salvation of souls than anything to do with our comfort, convenience or suc-

> *We forget that God does some of His best work in man when he is broken and weak.*

cess." Joni is a lady with very little comfort or convenience, and she was absolutely correct when she spoke about God's purpose as He works through our lives.

We look around us and observe that people living worldly lives experience adversity and prosperity in proportionally similar degrees. Perhaps we even wonder if we are really very different in God's sight. After all, we encounter most of the same obstacles. So, what is the difference between us?

The difference is that we have the Spirit of God living in us and sustaining us. And God doesn't seem to let any of our suffering be wasted. He is always ready to work His *purpose* through us in those difficult circumstances.

WHOSE POWER IS IT?

We forget that God does some of His best work in man when he is broken and weak. We forget that it is not our abilities but His ability that makes things happen. It is not our power but His power that moves mountains.

As Paul was being readied for the ministry, he felt it was very important that his "thorn in the flesh" be removed. After all, he could be so much more effective without that hindrance. It would really cramp his style. But the Lord said, *"My power is made perfect in weakness"* (II

Corinthians 12:9). In other words, the Lord was saying, "Paul, it is not your power but my power working through you that will accomplish my purpose." It is not unusual for God to perform some of His best work in us when we have been broken. It is often at a time when we feel unqualified and unfit for exemplary service.

When Moses was young and agile, with polished speech, he felt well qualified to work God's purpose, and he killed an Egyptian guard. Moses had gone into action without God's blessing, and it all went wrong. The timing was not right. Man often tries to work God's purpose in his own way.

It was when Moses was old and broken—his polished speech gone—that the Lord found him qualified.

Peter felt strong, eager and able early in his service to the Lord. He was zealous and felt that his faith was so strong that he could withstand any circumstance. That was just before he denied Christ three times.

It was only after that great failure, when Peter was so broken, that Jesus could say, "*Feed my lambs.*" Perhaps at that point Jesus knew that Peter was now humble enough to have God's purpose worked in him.

> *Satan seemed to believe that every man had his price.*

God also saw fit to work His purpose through a man named Job. In Job's case, God wanted to show Satan that some of the human race could and would remain faithful—even in the face of adversity. Satan seemed to believe that every man had his price. He thought that given enough loss, enough pain, enough humiliation, man would decide that God is not really there. In some cases man does think that.

Man is somewhat prone to think that becoming a believer means that God will shield him from the really painful circumstances of life. Some are even encouraged to believe that financial circumstances will improve if they become Christians. Such theology is false, because God never taught such ideas in His Word. It is much more than financial success that makes a believer joyful.

Like Job, most of us do not understand our disasters. Like Job, we do not usually know what God is doing when He works in our lives. However, Job's story has enormous implications for us, because it gave us a clear glimpse into Satan's agenda and the lengths to which he will go to separate us from God.

TOO ORDINARY

As Christians living in a time of moral and spiritual decline, do we believe that God is actually doing something through our lives? Sometimes we live as if we do not. Often, we tend to live our lives at a pace that does not make room for any *purpose* of God. We are just too consumed with our own purposes—and our purposes are far from singular!

Some of us just feel too ordinary to think that God might want to use our lives. What would it take to convince us that God wants to work His purpose through us?

What do we expect Him to do? Do we think that we must have a glowing resume to impress Him?

We tend to think that if God wants to use us, He will give us talent or ability so powerful that it will grab us and propel us into action. We expect Him to give us star power! We expect Him to give us fame and fortune—or at least significance!

God did bless some people with astonishing gifts. Mozart's talent was so pervasive that he could not bear to hear someone play a piece of mediocre music. He found himself rushing forward, taking over the keyboard and embellishing the music, adding whatever was needed to make that music a masterpiece. His gift consumed him.

> *Our gifts may seem so insignificant to us that we may never claim them.*

Few people have that level of talent. In view of Mozart's life, we might not really desire that level of genius. In fact very few exceedingly gifted people use their gifts to serve God.

The gifts that most of us have may not be all consuming or overpowering. Nevertheless, God has given each of us certain abilities. Our gifts may seem so insignificant to us that we may never claim them. They may seem too mundane to have any value. If our gift is not athletic ability or musical ability or creativity, we may decide that God did not favor us with a gift.

ACCOUNTABILITY

God is the one who supplies our abilities, and He is the one who initiates the opportunities to match those abilities. Like Esther, perhaps we are in this country *"for such a time as this."* Perhaps God has chosen you to be a strong, green tree amid the flying sparks of the raging fire. God supplies the ability needed for the opportunity given. It has been said that ability plus opportunity equals responsibility. The word "responsible" means that someone is accountable or answerable for something. We are accountable to God.

We may feel so overwhelmed and powerless by the spiritual decline in our world that we can't envision a role for ourselves. But God does not give a responsibility without supplying the power.

In the parable of the talents in Matthew 25:14, 15, the word *"talent"* referred to currency, but that currency was distributed *"according to their abilities"* (verse 15). The master knew what ability each servant had. The passage said, *"Again it will be like a man going on a journey, who called his servants and entrusted his property to them. To one he gave five talents of money, to another two talents, and to another one talent, each according to his ability."*

The servant who did not prosper seemed to believe that he had been given insufficient ability to administer his responsibility. He may have been like many of us who think that if we don't have star power, we have no ability. The reasonable conclusion is, "If I have no ability, then I have no responsibility." We think if God had made us like Moses or David, then He could expect us to do what they did.

Most Bible characters were not powerful in themselves. They were exemplary because they allowed themselves to be used for God's *purpose*. Their successful feats came as a result of God's power—just as He is with us in our

> *Most Bible characters were not powerful in themselves. They were exemplary because they allowed themselves to be used for God's purpose.*

service to Him. Did they have credentials? Ridiculous! One was a young shepherd boy when God was ready to use him, and the other was an old and broken shepherd. God can do great things through any of us when we allow ourselves to be used by Him.

We tend to think just like that servant in the parable, "Lord, you can't hold me accountable. I'm not responsible, because you gave me no ability to be a great servant in your kingdom." What do we expect God to do in order to make us productive for His purpose?

Perhaps we expect Him to give us genius so that our service will be the centerpiece of the kingdom. We don't want some menial talent like visiting the sick, sending cards, or being a good parent. Napoleon was once asked what could be done to make France a greater nation. He replied, "Give us better mothers." But we say, "Surely, Lord, you don't consider motherhood a special ability. No one would ever think that I am doing anything if that is all that I do! Here, Master, just take that one little old talent back. I want to be responsible for something more significant than that!"

Such thinking shows the influence of that raging fire in our world. The world says that being a servant isn't a powerful thing to do. That is the opposite of the teaching of Jesus. We can be very misguided by the opinions of the world.

Life will teach us that if we want more possibilities in life, then we must make the most of those small everyday opportunities that God gives us. If we do that, we will soon be amazed at how the opportunities multiply. The master in the parable gave more opportunities to the servant who made the most of the opportunities that he had been given.

So if we can't do the little "one-talent" things, we certainly can't do the really great things. One of my most memorable teachers would say, "Now, girls, if you can't wash your husband's socks and keep house in an ordinary one bedroom apartment, you won't be able to do it if he builds you a mansion."

In Matthew 25:28, the master said, *"Take the talent from him and give it to the one who has ten talents. For everyone who has will be given more, and he will have an abundance."* The man who had been given five talents of currency was given more, because he had shown that he was willing to make the most of his opportunities.

The one-talent person was called "worthless," because he denied that God had given him potential for service. His thinking was very familiar, "If I don't have the potential to do something really significant, then God is unfair and unjust."

GIFTS OF POWER

> *We expect Him to make us magically a bright and shining light before we have lifted a hand to light our own little candle.*

What do we expect of God? We expect Him to make us magically a bright and shining light before we have lifted a hand to light our own little candle. To realize what God has given us, we need to draw a little closer in our relationship with Him and to really understand what God has already done for us. The truth is, we are always powerless, but in relationship with our Lord, powerful things will happen.

We must learn to appreciate the purpose of God. We should realize that all our hurry and scurry may have nothing to do with His real purpose for our lives. God's gifts are not always straightforward or obvious.

There was once a young man who was about to graduate from high school. He very much wanted a car as a graduation gift, and he and his father went out frequently to look at prospective purchases.

On the day of his graduation, his father handed his son a small wrapped package. The boy was shocked and disappointed but opened the package. He thought perhaps it was keys to the car, but it was a Bible!

Feeling hurt and angry, the young graduate threw the Bible to the ground. It was not the gift he wanted! He left and never spoke to his father or saw him again.

Many years later, his father died, and his mother begged the son to come home for the funeral. He finally agreed reluctantly to come. While browsing through books in his father's study, he came across the Bible that had destroyed his relationship with his father. As he slowly fanned through its pages a piece of paper fell out and drifted to the floor. He picked it up and found it to be a check. The check was made out to him and dated on the date of his graduation many years earlier. It was made out for the price of that new car that he had wanted. That special gift had been there all the time!

God's best gifts are sometimes missed because of our worldly desires. In our humanness, we may think that God has given us nothing because we appreciate only the material things and surface stuff. Being distracted by the world's values can cause us to miss the real blessing. The smoke of that raging fire may be blinding us.

The blessing that God really wants to give us is not wrapped up with a pretty bow but is sometimes tucked just out of view—not to be realized unless we come to know our Father better. Our relationship with our Father may be too dysfunctional to withstand any misunderstanding, disappointment, or pain. We

> *We need to draw a little closer so that we don't miss our blessings.*

need to draw a little closer so that we don't miss our blessings.

Even the disciples of Jesus looked through human eyes and could not comprehend the gift of power that was theirs because of their relationship with Jesus. In Mark 8:14-21, when Jesus had just fed the four thousand, the disciples gathered seven baskets full of scraps. They followed Jesus to the other side, but they had a little memory lapse; they forgot their leftovers.

Jesus said to them, *"Be careful. Watch out for the yeast of the Pharisees and that of Herod."* (Jesus had spiritual concerns for his followers.) The followers, however, were thinking of physical matters, and they presumed that Jesus was unhappy with them because they had forgotten the "doggie bag."

Jesus was aware of their discussion and asked them, *"Why are you talking about having no bread? Do you still not see and understand? Are your hearts hardened? Do you have eyes but fail to see and ears but fail to hear?"*

Jesus was not focusing on their forgetfulness but on their inability to get beyond their worldliness. The disciples were missing their blessing. Jesus was empowering them, but they could not see their great blessing.

Jesus could easily take care of their tangible, mundane necessities—like bread. He wanted them to realize that His gifts were better than mere worldly necessities, but the disciples were not yet ready to value the better gifts. So often, that is our problem too.

These disciples were about to experience having God's purpose worked through them in astounding ways.

When Jesus warned them to be careful of the yeast, He was urging them to avoid being prideful and puffed up like the Pharisees. They must never think that those wonders they were about to perform were done through their own power.

The apostles were so ordinary—not one Mozart in the crowd. If they had been unusually gifted, there would have been even more danger that they would credit themselves instead of God. It isn't that God is adverse to the idea of working His purpose through a genius—in fact, He probably does! But genius is much more tempted to credit self.

The disciples were so ordinary that they probably often felt very inadequate as they fumbled and stumbled along side Jesus. Scripture makes it clear that the people through whom God worked His purpose were neither perfect nor infallible. No man is.

All that He needs from us is a willing heart—and that has always been the difficult part.

But the characteristic that marked these people was the one that we need. They would endure hardship, illness, persecution, and being ordinary—and never quit! Very significant things happened through these people—things that are remembered in Scripture.

A WILLING HEART

What should we expect of God when the fire is roaring and the ways of the world seem to be winning? We should expect that He knows exactly what can be done through our lives to work His purpose. God is powerful enough for both of us, and He can accomplish things that we might view as being impossible. All that He needs from us is a willing heart—and that has always been the difficult part.

When Moses drew a little closer to that burning bush, he found that God was ready to use him. "Why now?" thought Moses. There had been a time in his life when he was young and strong—well trained with polished speech—a man of the royal family! But now, well, he was just so ordinary. He could not possibly do anything for God's purpose.

The thing that was lacking in Moses at that time was a willing heart. Moses didn't want to go back. He didn't want to face the Pharaoh now that he was old and ordinary. Just like us, he wanted his own abilities to impress and pressure the Pharaoh. How could a plain shepherd with stammering speech do what God needed? Therefore, Moses was not willing to go. He didn't have a willing heart, because he thought that God needed gifted servants.

If God had needed Moses at his best, He would have used him many years earlier when Moses was ready and willing to act.

We think just exactly like Moses. How could God use someone who is struggling to make ends meet, can't carry a tune, not a Greek scholar, not very healthy, overweight, and trying to rear a bunch of children? How could God possibly use me? Sometimes we even wonder if He sees us at all—sometimes we wish He didn't. That describes the kind of person that God not only sees, but often uses in powerful ways.

Do you think that poor widow of Zarephath was someone who would have ever been on the evening news? She was so ordinary—so poor and broken that she was preparing her last cake of bread for herself and her son when God came and laid an opportunity right in her path. She was so helpless that God could use her. All that was needed was a willing heart, and she did have that. Her story was recorded for posterity in Scripture.

Perhaps our problem is that we forget what really is the purpose of God. There is something wonderful about that singular nature of God's purpose. It really does have to do with the salvation of souls! The whole saga of the Hebrews in the Old Testament, as well as the entire New Testament, marched doggedly toward one all-consuming goal. God's purpose has always been to save as many souls as possible. II Peter 3:9 spoke of the preciousness of salvation, *"He is patient with you, not wanting anyone to perish, but everyone to come to repentance."*

His purpose is not about our satisfying lifestyles. It is not about our right to happiness or prosperity. It is about being sure that we get to go to heaven and take with us as many souls as possible. In many of our difficult and unwanted circumstances, the hand of God is busily working His purpose in us. God's purpose does not change, even though Satan stokes his fire of immorality and spiritual decline.

In II Corinthians 4:7, Paul referred to us as *"jars of clay."*
The properties of clay are such that they become mud if
they get wet, or they may begin to crumble if exposed to
weather for a lengthy period of time. In that state, clay is
a rather weak and worthless substance. When it is heated
to the proper temperature, it shrinks and hardens. It no
longer becomes soft or crumbly when the rain comes.

Like clay, we are weak and fragile. But Paul said in II
Corinthians 4:7, *"But we have this treasure in jars of clay to
show that this all-surpassing power is from God and not from
us."* He was saying that we are like clay jars with no
power in ourselves, but God has *made His light to shine in
our hearts* (verse 6). So when we have been exposed to the
heat of life's adversity, we become more durable. In his
own difficult times, Paul was able to say in verse 8, *"We
are hard pressed on every side, but not crushed; perplexed, but
not in despair; persecuted, but not abandoned; struck down, but
not destroyed."*

In a time of moral and spiritual decline, our lives will
be more satisfying if our purpose is the same as that of the
Father. Think about this carefully in your quiet time and
pray about it. The goals that we set for our families sometimes have nothing to do with God or His purpose. Are
we living for our own purposes and just hoping that God
will follow along at a distance? When our goals harmo-
nize with God's purpose, we are able to look at the raging
fire from a different perspective—from the perspective
that the best is yet to come for those who remain faithful.

STRANGERS IN THIS PLACE

"This fellow came here as an alien, now he wants to play judge."

Genesis 19:9

When we are truly sojourners in a foreign land, it is almost impossible for us to blend in with those who are native to that land. Most people will know that we are aliens. We stand out like a sore thumb. Even if we are able to speak their language, we still have a recognizable accent. We do things differently; we think differently and usually dress differently. Any sense of danger is heightened because we are unaccustomed to their method of handling problems. Not being able to understand their language causes confusion.

While spending a few months in Romania, an electrical fire erupted in the apartment building where we were staying. We were awakened by the sound of frightened voices, but we couldn't understand what they were saying. We heard fire trucks arriving and decided that we should stop gawking and take action. It was time to get dressed and get out of that building. In any language, a fire means danger!

Today, there is a fire raging in our homeland. Because we consider the United States to be our home, we may not feel 'quite so threatened because we know what is happening. We mistakenly forget that even here there is a sense in which we are still pilgrims. Here, we understand the language, and we understand the customs, but we may be even more vulnerable to the fire. Familiar fires are less frightening. In certain refineries, fires burn constantly, and no one thinks much about it. Yet those fires are very hot and can be deadly. This sinister fire of godlessness that threatens our land burns twenty-four hours a day. It is so familiar that we are tempted to disregard it.

Occasionally, some fiery explosion gets our attention, and we wish that we could do something to turn the tide. It is obvious that this place through which we are sojourning needs some serious reformation. With every fiber of our being, we want to cry out against our immoral pagan culture. We wonder how our land could have become so wicked.

However, we pilgrims cannot hang our hope and joy on the prospect of a righteous country. We need not expect that there will be godly leaders or justice in

> *We pilgrims cannot hang our hope and joy on the prospect of a righteous country.*

government. That may be disappointing; however, we should remember that we are on our way to the Promised Land, and we are not there yet! There is no place on this earth that is going to be the Promised Land. It never has been—even in the "good old days." It never will be.

ABRAHAM LIVED AMONG THE UNGODLY

Abraham's life was spent living as a stranger and a pilgrim in foreign lands. Abraham and his tribe of followers were our prototypes. In Hebrews 11:9 we read, *"By faith, he made his home in the Promised Land like a stranger in a foreign country; he lived in tents as did Isaac and Jacob."*

Abraham found himself living among people who did not share his respect for God's authority. The raging fire of immorality always blazed just outside his tent. Those pagans put their trust in other gods and lived very sinful lives. The kings in whose land Abraham traveled were not moral men. There was an obvious swath between Abraham and the pagans, and it was there because Abraham kept faith with his convictions. Perhaps Abraham felt the urge to clean up the decadence of those lands, but there is no indication that he ever attempted to do so. He had interaction with the kings of those lands but wasn't attempting to make social changes. He just steadily stayed the course, trying to be a man of God.

> *He just steadily stayed the course, trying to be a man of God.*

Abraham's allegiance was to a King that no one in those lands knew or understood. Abraham was principled and powerful in a way that must have seemed very mysterious to those pagans.

COULD THIS BE THE PROMISED LAND?

Canaan was called "the Promised Land," not because it was such a wonderful place, but because it was the place that had been promised by God to Abraham for His people. There was much about Canaan that made it an unlikely place for a land of promise—especially its inhabitants. It was a narrow strip of land, traveled by armies on their way to battle. It was also a trade route for merchants.

Although Abrahams's descendants did become as numerous as the stars in the skies, the original patriarchs did not live to take possession of Canaan. In Hebrews 11, we read that those faithful patriarchs really were hoping for a better prize than physical Canaan. In very symbolic language, Hebrew 11:16 said, *"Instead, they were longing for a better country—a heavenly one."* Their heavenly homeland would require no firebreaks, because there would be no raging fire there. All its citizens would be people of God.

Abraham and his people had always endured the contempt of those around them. Foreigners were viewed with suspicion, and they were humiliated.

As Christians we share some of the experiences of Abraham and his followers. We find ourselves trying to mend the flaws in the social fabric of our world—something Abraham did not do. In recent years, organizations have sprung up hoping to gain political leverage for Christian causes. Actually, they have had very limited success, and Christianity seems to have been placed in the same category as any other lobbying group. In reality, we, too, are "looking for a better country—a heavenly one." This world will never be that country.

LAW VS. A TRANSFORMED HEART

Even as pilgrims, we can have an impact on many individual lives as we sojourn here, but that impact comes not by force. God can use us to work His purpose in powerful ways, but for Christians to move into the political arena sometimes seems to be counterproductive to the cause of Christ. Public theology demands a clarity that the citizens of the world cannot tolerate, and therefore the teachings of Christ become compromised in the interest of political correctness.

The real power of the Christian cause will never come from government. The power of Christianity to transform comes from God, and that transformation happens one heart at a time. The hope that sweeping legislation will right all the wrongs that engulf our society is a mirage. Laws will not effectively change lives. It is the power of God's Word that brings about that transformation.

As pilgrims, our struggle against immorality and violence is really a battle with Satan. We can rail against him, march in the streets, pass laws, or throw money at him, but it is usually the positive approach that will do the greatest damage to Satan. Jesus taught us to use a more positive

> *Laws will not effectively change lives.*

approach. It is not just a matter of removing evil; it is filling that empty place where evil had been. If something good fails to replace the evil, the evil will return. Jesus taught that lesson in Matthew 12:43 when He said,

When an evil spirit comes out of a man, it goes through arid places seeking rest and does not find it. Then it says, "I will return to the house I left." When it arrives, it finds the house unoccupied, swept clean and put in order. Then it goes and takes with it seven other spirits more wicked than itself, and they go in and live there. And the final condition of that man is worse than the first.

This story shows why mere laws cannot effect the transformation that we pilgrims seek. It isn't enough to require that evil vacate the premises. A life that fills its house with good works must consume that vacant space, lest sin return and overpower its victim.

THE POSITIVE APPROACH

The positive approach may be more difficult than merely complaining about wrongdoing. We would much rather have laws passed to prohibit evil. Jesus said, *"Love your enemies and pray for those who persecute you"* (Matthew 5:44). Could we consider praying for the Hollywood moguls who produce movies that glorify wicked behavior? Perhaps we could ask God

> *Many social ills can be improved when attitudes are sweetened.*

to give them a change of heart. Could we pray for local and district judges and the Supreme Court? Perhaps God might supply wisdom for their decision making process. Surely we don't think that government has more power than God does to stay the forces of Satan in our world.

During His earthly ministry Jesus didn't tackle the social ills of His day—even though there were many ills. Slavery was prevalent, but there is no record of His trying to correct that wrong. In fact, Paul later wrote to the Ephesian church, suggesting that becoming a Christian would not change social conditions. In Ephesians 6:5, he wrote, *"Slaves, obey your earthly masters with respect and fear."* Changed hearts moved men to alter their behavior, and some masters became kinder to their slaves. Many social ills can be improved when attitudes are sweetened.

We are aliens in a world that has devalued human life. Many children are murdered before they have had opportunity to live outside the womb. Others are born into one-parent dwellings, and sometimes there is almost no parent. Such children have no understanding of love and relationships, so they grow up with aberrant behavior. Jesus didn't teach us to bemoan such circumstances, He taught us to do something about them. He said that we should feed the hungry and care for widows and orphans. If we actively took the initiative to assist and encourage

> *Jesus lived like a pilgrim and showed us that even pilgrims can have an impact on the world.*

helpless children, we would be more effective than any law passed by government. Taking the initiative to fill the void would be more in keeping with Jesus' plan of action.

To combat abortion some groups have set up Pregnancy Centers across the country. No one knows whether these centers can be credited, but the abortion rate has decreased. Jesus' approach was to do something caring to right injustice. Jesus lived like a pilgrim and showed us that even pilgrims can have an impact on the world.

CHRISTIANS ARE ALIENS

The Lord views His people as aliens or pilgrims in this place. These words come from the Greek words *paroikos* and *parepidemos*, and they refer to someone who is a temporary resident.

Referring to the church in I Peter 2:11, Peter said, *"Dear friends, I urge you as aliens and strangers in the world, to abstain from evil desires that war against your soul."* Webster says that an alien is one who belongs to another people. Secondly, he says that the word, "alien," means strange and not natural. Those definitions rather accurately describe God's people throughout the ages. The Christian who lives as the Lord intended will live in contrast to the ways of the world. The world views the faithful Christian as being rather strange and unnatural.

Although we know that we are God's people, we have difficulty remembering that we are only passing through this place. In reality our stay here is very brief. The writer in First Chronicles 29:15 said, *"We are aliens and strangers in your sight, as were all our forefathers. Our days on earth are like a shadow."* A shadow is a very fleeting phenomenon. Its very existence is dependent upon the movement of the sun. Our existence is also a very temporary thing!

Even though the Lord refers to us as aliens, strangers, or pilgrims, He is in no way suggesting anarchy. Quite the contrary! He instructs us to obey the laws of the land and also calls us to obey a higher standard of laws than any earthly laws.

Jesus taught that we have obligation to pay taxes when He said in Luke 20:25, *"Give to Caesar what is Caesar's."* Jesus also complied with the demands of a tax assessor when He obliged Peter to catch that fish with a coin in its mouth in order to pay the tax. Regardless of whether the tax was just, Jesus complied.

Furthermore, we are taught to respect those who are in authority over us—even though our first allegiance is to God. In Acts 23:5, Paul repeated a law of God from

Exodus 22:28: *"Do not speak evil about the ruler of your people."* Later, in writing to the Christians in Rome, Paul spoke at length about our being in submission to governing authorities. In Romans 13:1, he said, *"The authorities that exist have been established by God. Consequently, he who rebels against the authority is rebelling against what God has instituted..."* Peter even wrote to persecuted Christians in I Peter 2:17 saying, *"Show proper respect to everyone: Love the brotherhood of believers, fear God, honor the king."*

It is not unusual to see injustice in matters of government, and Christianity may never be treated fairly in the governing process. We cannot understand what God is doing when certain rulers come to power. The Jews certainly couldn't imagine why a king like Nebuchadnezzar was given such incredible power. It is especially difficult to resist speaking against a ruler who is evil. It must have been almost impossible for those mistreated believers to whom Peter wrote. Nevertheless, there is every reason to believe that Paul's and Peter's admonitions apply to present day "aliens and pilgrims" in the church.

> *It is especially difficult to resist speaking against a ruler who is evil.*

When we are aliens, we must endure whatever difficulties or adversities are indigenous to the land in which we sojourn. If food is scarce, we stand in bread lines. If there is draught, we limit our water usage. If there is crime in the streets, we may become victims. If there is sickness, we will likely become ill. In this foreign land there will certainly be physical death, but because we are aliens, death will be different for us. Death for us will be as if we are finally crossing the border into our homeland.

HOW TO LIVE AS AN ALIEN

In the Old Testament when God allowed the Jews to be taken into Babylonian captivity by Nebuchadnezzar, they literally became strangers in a foreign land. About ten thousand of Judah's leading citizens were taken to Babylon, but God intended to eventually bless those aliens. So He continued to speak to them through prophets. Jeremiah was the Lord's true prophet, but there were false prophets too.

The false prophets did what all false prophets tend to do; they told the people what they wanted to hear. In Jeremiah 27, the word of the Lord came through Jeremiah saying that those false prophets were prophesying lies by telling the people that they would not have to serve Nebuchadnezzar, king of Babylon. Of course, they were already in Babylonian captivity, but the false prophets were saying, "Don't even unpack your bags!" They wanted to convince the people that the Lord would end their captivity very soon.

When God's true prophet Jeremiah spoke, he didn't paint such a sunny scenario. He told the Jews that the Lord said they would have to serve Nebuchadnezzar, king of Babylon, and his people, not for a year or two, but for seventy years!

Which of these prophets do you suppose the Jews wanted to believe? The people of our culture today tend

The people in our culture today tend to believe the one who looks the best or promises the most.

to believe the one who looks the best or promises the most. The people of Judah were no exception. The aliens wanted to go home and were living as if they expected to be in Babylon for only a short time. Eventually, God disposed of the false prophets and gave instructions through Jeremiah to the exiles.

The Lord's instructions for aliens living in a foreign land are given in Jeremiah 29:4ff. Since we also are considered aliens, perhaps these instructions have meaning for us. First, the Lord said, *"Build your houses and settle down."* It was in their best interest to provide shelter for their families and live as if they were at home. Their allegiance was not really to Nebuchadnezzar, but they would have to serve him. They were to "settle down" and not be in a state of unrest.

In the New Testament, the "aliens" who made up the church of Thessalonica were also told how to live, and it sounded somewhat similar to those in Babylon. Paul said in I Thessalonians 4:11, *"Make it your ambition to lead a quiet life, to mind your own business and to work with your hands, just as we told you, so that your daily life may win the respect of outsiders and so that you will not be dependent on anybody."* Such a life would gain a good reputation for the alien and improve his opportunity to influence others.

Second, the Lord said the exiles in Babylon should *"Plant gardens and eat the fruit."* The Lord didn't want them to be dependent, lest they become slaves. It was the upper class Jew who had been taken into exile, and they were very capable people. It is likely that the king thought they could make valuable contribution to his kingdom. God favored these aliens and eventually would bring them home, but for now they were to settle down and be productive.

The third message that God had for the aliens was very interesting. He said, *"Increase in number."* He told them to marry and have children, and then He explicitly told them, *"Do not decrease."* In difficult times it is human wisdom to resist bringing children into the world, but it was not God's formula for aliens. Even when the children of Israel were aliens in Egypt, they grew in number. There were so many of them that the Pharaoh became uncomfortable and made them slaves.

God multiplied those Hebrews like the sand on the seashore and like the stars in the heavens. God's people have always been in the minority while large numbers of others are willing to become fuel for the raging fire of immorality and godlessness. Larger numbers of godly people would enable believers to encourage each other, and perhaps dampen the raging fire. Even today, God's people should not decrease in number. Not only should we have chil-

> *God's people have always been in the minority while large numbers of others are willing to become fuel for the raging fire of immorality and godlessness.*

dren, we should reach out to those in the world who need a spiritual rebirth.

The fourth message to the aliens in Babylon was, *"Seek the peace and prosperity of the city to which I have carried you. Pray to the Lord for it, because if it prospers, that will benefit you."* The Lord has always taught His people to pray for an environment more conducive to living righteous lives. In the New Testament, Paul wrote in I Timothy 2:1, 2, *"I urge then, first of all, that requests, prayers, intercession and thanksgiving be made for everyone—for kings and all those in authority, that we may live peaceful and quiet lives in all godliness and holiness."* As aliens, we should remember to pray for those in authority, because their decisions will affect our peace and prosperity.

While we are pilgrims and aliens in this place, we will also need to be cautious lest we become captives here. It would be a mistake to become too enamored by the glitter of this world. Some aliens like their foreign land so much that they find themselves applying for permanent citizenship. We may begin to feel so much at home that we want to stay.

That may have been Lot's problem; he and his family had become too much "at home" in Sodom. When Lot and Abram separated, Scripture said that Lot *"pitched his tents near Sodom."* Later, he seemed to have a home in Sodom. It was not that Lot had become wicked; it was that he had become attached! His family had known that place as their home. As for Lot, he was miserable, but not troubled enough to leave. In II Peter 2:7-9, Peter said:

And if He (God) rescued Lot, a righteous man, who was distressed by the filthy lives of lawless men (for that righteous man living among them day after day was tormented in his righteous soul by the lawless deeds he saw and heard)—if this is so, then the Lord knows how to rescue godly men from trials and to hold the unrighteous for the day of judgment.

Like Lot, we find ourselves distressed by blatant lawlessness around us. We shake our heads and lament the condition of our world. Still, we stay right in Sodom, and sometimes we are guilty of indulging ourselves in some of the perverse offerings of the entertainment industry. We consider this place to be our home, and we allow its culture to dictate to our families. If the Lord came and offered to rescue us,

> *If the Lord came and offered to rescue us, would we hesitate?*

would we hesitate? There was obvious hesitation on the part of Lot and his family. The prospective sons-in-law thought the whole thing was a joke and didn't even consider leaving. But Genesis 19:16 said, *"When he (Lot) hesitated, the men grasped his hand and the hands of his wife and of his two daughters and led them safely out of the city, for the Lord was merciful to them."* The two angels had to take hold and tug in order to get them out of Sodom. If the Lord had not been merciful, they would have perished there.

Even after they were out of Sodom, we heard Lot pleading with the angels not to take them to the mountains. It was too far! He persuaded them to let him go to Zoar, a small town nearby. There was something about the plains around Sodom and Gomorrah that had capti-vated that family. It isn't easy to remain aloof while living in the world. Everyone knows that Mrs. Lot looked back. Of course, none of us would do that. Her home, her pos-sessions, and her memories were going up in flames. She had become attached to Sodom. So that pillar of salt has stood as a reminder to us that we should keep our alien status and never let the world possess us.

It is possible that Lot no longer considered himself an alien in Sodom, even though he was tormented by its wickedness. However, the men of Sodom still viewed him as an alien. Those who abandon their lives to the ravages of the raging fire always scoff at the righteous person. The men of Sodom said, *"This fellow came here as an alien, and now he wants to play the judge!"* Lot had no influence among those ungodly people. He would always be a stranger, because his allegiance was to the God that they did not know.

It has been told that there was once a missionary returning home from having worked in the mission field for many years. It happened that he was riding on the same train as the President of the United States. The President was returning from a pleasure trip, and when the train stopped in the city for the President to get off the train, a very large crowd was waiting and cheering his arrival. Eventually the train moved on, finally arriving in the missionary's hometown. As he departed the train, there was only one person there to meet him. It was the local minister.

The missionary told him of the President's grand reception at the train station and noted the contrast with his own lonely arrival. The minister said, "Well, that is very easy to explain. You see, you're not home yet!"

There will not likely be a grand reception for us in a place that is not our home. In Jeremiah 29:10, the Lord concluded His message to those in Babylonian captivity by saying, "*When seventy years are completed for Babylon, I will come to you and fulfill my gracious promise to bring you back...*" Seven or seventy are numbers used in Hebrew to symbolize fullness or completeness. This promise that God gave to the aliens in Babylon has even greater implication for us. For them, it meant the hope of returning to Judah. But for us, it means when the fullness of time has come, the Lord will take us to our real home where we will no longer be strangers. A raging fire will eventually consume this world. But we will be in our homeland with full citizenship, and our reception will be beyond description!

COUNT IT ALL JOY

"But let all who take refuge in you be glad, let them sing for joy."

Psalm 5:11, 12

It was the apostle Paul who demonstrated that it is absolutely possible to face hardship and still have joy. He sang praises to God in his jail cell. But it was James who wrote in James 1:2, *"Count it pure joy, my brothers, when you face trials of many kinds, because you know that the testing of your faith develops perseverance."* Joy does not mean that the raging fire poses no threat. It doesn't mean that God's people will be free from the pain of its consequences. Our joy comes because we know that the real battle is over, and we won! Jesus has risen from the dead, and our sal-

> *Our joy comes because we know that the real battle is over, and we won!*

vation has been assured. No matter what happens to us in this world, it cannot change that fact. No one can take that hope from us. We can give it away, but no one can take it from us.

Today, the raging fire of moral and spiritual decline threatens to defeat us, but James said, *"Count it all joy."* Why should that give us any joy? Perhaps a period such as the one in which we live will refine our faith. Our faith has not been tested very much in this country. Having real enemies confront our faith will either strengthen it or destroy it. Experiencing a raging fire that opposes our faith will separate the tall, green trees from the dry under-brush.

Sometimes, it is when we have endured long and difficult struggles that we emerge stronger for the experience. It may be when we have watched the long, gradual deterioration of someone we love. Sometimes, it is our own health problems. It may be family trouble, financial disaster, or problems with our children. It may be when we have lost favor with an employer because of our faith. When thick, murky darkness settles around us like a cover, we may feel helpless and almost defeated. Yet, such adversities equip us for other battles in life, and that is reason for joy.

Most people still think it strange that James would say, *"Count it all joy."* The Bible scholar William Barclay explained, "The effect of testing rightly borne is strength to bear still more and to conquer in still harder battles." Mr. Barclay was talking about the way we carry our burdens, and he was suggesting that we not dwell on the dark side of life's circumstances. If we decide not to be defeated, we will keep pushing onward. When we keep going, we gradually begin to learn that there is much more to be gained by pressing on rather than quitting. We can benefit from struggling through hardships, because it prepares us for the next trouble that comes our way.

THE FETAL POSITION
There is, of course, an alternative. We can lie down and curl up in a fetal position. We all have some vulnerability to that particular solution. Throughout the years, there have always been those who chose the fetal approach to their problems. That approach requires nothing of us—we don't have to struggle or fight the battle. We only have to feel the pain. We just let the enemy take control without our resistance.

The fetal position is the way we were in the womb—safe and secure. Maybe the thumb was even in the mouth. There were no hurdles to jump and no valleys of despair. So, when we are jolted by the realities of life with its raging fire and flying sparks, the easy approach would be to retire to the safety of the womb. But where is the joy? In the womb, man's life is in limbo, there is no light, no hope, and no purpose.

REASON TO GO ON

When we are tempted to surrender to the struggles of trying be a Christian in a pagan world, we need to strengthen our determination to continue our walk of faith until Jesus comes or until we die. To take that goal seriously will give us reason to go on. People who can see no reason to go on will soon find themselves too weak to make the effort.

> *People who see no reason to go on will soon find themselves too weak to make the effort.*

In Luke 13:32, 33, Jesus showed a tenacious spirit by sending a response to Herod, and in that message, He said, *"Go tell that fox, I will drive out demons and heal people today and tomorrow and on the third day, I will reach my goal. In any case, I must keep going today and tomorrow and the next day…"*

Jesus had a reason to keep going; He said that He had a goal. He had decided that He could endure trials, temptation, and persecution day after day, because He had a reason to do it. He even knew that before He reached His goal, He would suffer the worst possible pain and humiliation. Still, He pressed on.

Paul also knew that he had reason to pursue life fully, and he was prone to mention his goal. In Philippians 3:14, he said, "*I press on toward the goal to win the prize.*" In II Corinthians 5:9, Paul said, "*So we make it our goal to please Him.*" He knew that there was every reason to keep going. Each adversity just reinforced his resolve.

People often decide that they have no reason to keep going. When we decide that there are no goals out there, we lose our incentive. At that point we tend to become very negative, and that attitude creates its own misery. Life need not be that way for any of us. There are people in very uncomfortable circumstances who continue to see purpose and positives in their lives.

One lady whose legs were paralyzed had her circumstances further complicated by poverty. Her husband lost his job, and they lost their home. They finally managed to rent a small house but had no car. There was no way to get her to the doctor. One day a church donated a van to them. As her husband rolled her out in her wheelchair to see the new van, she was heard to say, "Honey, aren't we just the luckiest people in the world?"

It only depends on how we choose to look at things. Some of us have been greatly blessed and still think life has been too hard for us.

The focus of the hummingbird versus. that of the buzzard should teach us that it is only a matter of what we try to find. The little hummingbird spends its time in search of beautiful flowers in order to drink their sweet nectar. The buzzard soars about trying to spot some decaying carcass in order to devour the rotting meat. The little hummingbird cares nothing for rotting flesh; it only looks for what is sweet and beautiful.

How much more joy will be in our lives if we can appreciate what is sweet and beautiful! There is nothing sweet or beautiful in that raging fire of spiritual decline in our land. We should not allow ourselves to be captivated by any of its participants. That fire can change our perception about life's purpose and can cloud our goals.

In commenting on the subject of joy as it was discussed in James 1, William Barclay said, "By the way in which we meet every experience in life, we are either fitting or unfitting ourselves for the task that God meant us to do." In one of our earlier chapters, we examined the fact that God does have purpose for each of us. We also looked at the Greek word *teleios* as it was applied to Jesus. The word showed that Jesus became "perfect," because He carried out the purpose for which He came to earth.

Our trials can grow our perseverance, and each of those trying experiences may better equip us for God's purpose. However, if we allow difficult conditions to control us, we may

> *Our trials can grow our perseverance, and each of those trying experiences may better equip us for God's purpose.*

find ourselves unqualified for the purpose for which God would like to use us.

Paul used various forms of the word "joy" numerous times in his writings as he urged Christians to rejoice in the Lord. In Romans 5:3, he said, "...*we also rejoice in our sufferings, because we know that suffering produces perseverance.*"

The joy of which Paul spoke is an emotion similar to the way an athlete appreciates a hard workout. He knows that he is building muscle so that when the real contest comes, he will be equipped to do well. We have joy in knowing that hardship, sorrow, strain, and stress have built spiritual muscle to equip us for uphill battles in life.

REJOICE ANYWAY

Paul lived what he preached as he persisted in keeping the faith during frequent adversity. Acts 16 is probably the most graphic example of his joy in suffering. He and Silas were arrested and illegally beaten. Their bodies must have been a bloody mess. Even though they were probably stinging and aching from the pain of their severe flogging and having their feet being fastened in stocks, they were singing and praying.

In II Corinthians 6:10, Paul listed a whole series of afflictions that he had suffered and yet still lived hopefully. He said, "...*beaten, and yet not killed; sorrowful, yet always rejoicing; poor, yet making many rich; having nothing, and yet possessing everything.*" He pointed out the contrasts between the pain of our physical circumstances and the hopeful anticipation that resides in us spiritually when we can keep our eyes on the larger picture. When we remember the promise of our inheritance, we just might feel joy, even through our tears.

Isaiah once said in Isaiah 12:3, *"With joy, you will draw water from the springs of Salvation."* It is our promise of eternal life that allows joy to swell in our hearts.

> **When we remember the promise of our inheritance, we just might feel joy, even through our tears.**

Paul conducted himself as if his adversity were "all in a day's work." In Paul's heart, it was a matter of carrying out God's purpose for him. He was not about to curl up in a fetal position in that jail. He sang songs that helped to lift his spirits and his determination. When the authorities realized that they had beaten a Roman citizen, they were alarmed. They tried to have Paul and Silas released quietly, but Paul said, *"They beat us publicly without a trial, even though we were Roman citizens...and now do they want to get rid of us quietly? No! Let them come themselves and escort us"* (Acts 16:37). Paul reflected the kind of spirit that had determination, and he knew why he should not quit. Satan would never have the satisfaction of seeing him dispirited.

In 1996, there was a young man named Lance Armstrong who had everything going for him. He was a cyclist who was ranked seventh in the world. He had a two million-dollar contract to ride for a prestigious French team, and he was twenty-five years old.

Suddenly, he became ill. Tests were run, and he was diagnosed as having cancer that had spread to his lungs and abdomen. Immediately, he was given chemotherapy. His career and his life seemed to be finished. He was stunned! His life had changed so dramatically and so quickly.

Then, things got worse. Tumors were discovered in his brain! A neurosurgeon cut two circles about the size of a silver dollar in his head and removed the tumors. He was given about a thirty-percent chance for survival.

For many of us, that would have been the time for the fetal position, but not for Lance! Only a few months later, he began working out again. He did a few rides for charity. There was still something out there that he wanted to do. He had reason to keep going.

However, Lance had lost fifteen pounds of muscle. Cyclists are trained to push harder gears with larger muscles, but Lance would not be able to do that. His coach looked for and found another way. He tried using an easier gear but pedaled faster—one hundred to one hundred and ten revolutions per minute. It seemed to work!

He entered the competition for cycling's greatest prize—the Tour de France. He suffered through long, grueling mountain climbs. The competition had twenty stages and covered two thousand, two hundred and eighty-two miles. Lance Armstrong came in first in that race!

He has been an inspiration to cancer patients all over the world. He didn't really do all of that work in order to be an inspiration—although he is glad to have encouraged others. He did it because he had a goal. There was a prize out there that he wanted to win. So, he fought his way back from cancer and won the Tour de France.

Hardship was not a stranger to this young man. Many of his twenty-seven years had been spent overcoming hurdles. Cancer had been just one more obstacle in his course.

Unlike Lance Armstrong who had physical goals, we have spiritual goals. There are still similarities. Lance knew why he needed to double his effort to push on when everything seemed against him. We also know why we need to get back up after every defeat and never quit. We really should have even more incentive than Lance had, because our prize is infinitely more valuable.

Many trends in our culture may not bode well for Christians. We are vulnerable to any number of painful, unchangeable disasters. We should be thinking about our faith and what will enable us to endure no matter what happens. What is it that can remind us of the joy that we should have, even as we feel the sparks from the raging fire? It is the word of God!

> *We should be thinking about our faith and what will enable us to endure, no matter what happens.*

The entire 119th Psalm is devoted to exalting the word of God and the strength that it gives to our thirsty souls in time of trouble. In the midst of heartache, loss and pain, the psalmist said, *"Don't let my hopes be dashed."* That thought shows great insight into the human heart. In the midst of trial, the heart may begin to wonder, "Is this all there is? Nothing but this suffering?" So, the psalmist cried out to the Lord not to allow him to lose hope during hard times.

In Psalm 119:24, he said, *"Your statutes are my delights; they are my counselors."* We need to be faithful in our study of the Word so that it will be written on our hearts. It will remind us of our reason for pushing on toward the prize.

Psalm 119:71 even says, *"It was good for me to be afflicted, so that I might learn your decrees."* One of the positives about affliction is that it causes us to turn our attention to God and what He tells us in His Word. It is Scripture that is most often read in trying times.

The raging fire could grow so fierce that we don't have easy access to a Bible. Perhaps we would be wise to give our minds a workout, and memorize those scriptures that strengthen and encourage us the most. You probably have your own list, and here are a few other suggestions:

"The Lord is my strength and my shield; my heart trusts in him, and I am helped." Psalm 28:7

"Greater is He who is in you than he who is in the world." I John 4:4

"For nothing is impossible with God." Luke 1:37

"I consider that our present sufferings are not worth comparing with the glory that will be revealed in us." Romans 8:18

"God causes all things to work together for the good of those who love him, who have been called according to his purpose." Romans 8:28

"No temptation has seized you except what is common to man. And God is faithful; he will not let you be tempted beyond

what you can bear. But when you are tempted he will also provide a way out so that you can stand up under it."

I Corinthians 10:13

"Do not be anxious about anything, but in everything by prayer and petition, with thanksgiving present your requests to God." Philippians 4:6

"He is a shield to those who take refuge in Him." Proverbs 30:5

> *The trials of which James spoke were not tests designed to cause man to sin.*

With such passages written in our hearts, we may be strengthened to "count it all joy" when we face trials of many kinds. The trials of which James spoke were not tests designed to cause man to sin. These are trials intended to strengthen us, so that when the ways of the world seem to be winning, we are more likely to press on rather than become hopeless.

It is very much like being in training. If you can hike three miles the first day, perhaps you will be able to hike four miles the second day. Then, if the flying sparks from the raging fire land near you, you will find the strength to escape. The previous training would have supplied the stamina needed.

Abraham's walk with the Lord started with a rather difficult command from God. The Lord let it be known on day one that this journey was not for wimps. Indeed, Abraham was put to the test again and again. Still, the Lord always held out hope to him, and it kept him inspired. Likewise, the Lord has given us a promise that gives us hope.

For Abraham, it was such a long and complicated journey. One can almost hear Sarah ask, "Now, what is our reason for all this?"

And Abraham's reply, "Well, I am going to become the father of many nations."

Such conversations must have been quite confusing for Sarah since she had no children.

Most of us would have begun to doubt that there was really an inheritance. Then, after all the struggles and the birth of Isaac, God made the most unbelievable demand of Abraham. Take the life of this long awaited heir, Isaac. Many of us would have drawn the line right there, but Abraham was an experienced sufferer. His faith had already been refined by fire. He would remain faithful and hopeful.

Belief in the Lord is not something that overwhelms us, even as we attempt to resist it. It is a conscious decision that we make, based upon the evidence presented in the word of God. After our hearts are convicted, we undertake the commitment to live as He would have us live.

Satan will throw many obstacles in our paths. He will try to make us feel foolish. He will show us that most other folks don't share our convictions. It will require grit and determination to stay the course.

> *Many of us would have drawn the line right there, but Abraham was an experienced sufferer.*

Scripture suggests that God provides us a special measure of strength for the struggles if we commit ourselves to
His will. In Isaiah 40:27, the prophet asked Israel how
they could possibly think that God had no concern for the
"cause." In verse 29, he added, *"He gives strength to the
weary and increases the power of the weak."* Then, Isaiah really gave pause for reflection as he promised even more in
verses 30-31:

*Even youths grow tired and weary, and young men stumble
and fall.*

But those who hope in the Lord will renew their strength.

*They will soar on wings like eagles; they will run and not
grow weary,*

They will walk and not be faint.

God gives us something special when we decide to stay
the course. Scripture gave us glimpses of personal, individual assistance given to various individuals. In Joseph's
case, Genesis 39:2 said, *"The Lord was with Joseph, and he
prospered..."* Verses 20-21 said, *"But while Joseph was there
in prison, the Lord was with him; He showed him kindness and
granted him favor in the eyes of the prison warden."* It was the
Lord whose hand was at work. Joseph was neither
released from Egypt or prison at that point, but God was
taking care of Joseph's needs.

When Jesus was in great anguish as He prayed at the
Mount of Olives, we read in Luke 22:43, *"An angel from
heaven appeared to him and strengthened him."* Jesus was not
to be spared the crucifixion, but God was doing something to strengthen Him.

In Acts 7:55, 56, as Stephen was being stoned, the writer said, *"But Stephen, full of the Holy Spirit, looked up to heaven and saw the glory of God. 'Look,' he said, 'I see heaven open and the Son of Man standing at the right hand of God.'"* In each of these cases, the Father individually blessed His children with measures that would enable them to bear the adversity they faced.

The apostle Paul repeatedly gave the Lord credit for his endurance. He said in Philippians 4:13, *"I can do everything through him who gives me strength."*

Is there a positive side to our being allowed to bear heavy burdens in our Christian walk? Even earthly goals are valued primarily because so much commitment and diligence are required in order to achieve them. We grow when we encounter resistance. If we quit because of resistance, we lose everything.

It is said that a man once found the cocoon of a butterfly. He faithfully watched the cocoon until one day a small hole could be seen at one end. The man sat for hours watching the butterfly struggle to force his body though that small hole. It seemed that the butterfly was making very little progress and could go no further.

So, the man, feeling great pity for the poor butterfly, snipped the end off the cocoon with a pair of scissors. The butterfly very easily flopped itself out of the cocoon. But its body was swollen, and its wings were shriveled and small.

The man felt sure that in a few moments the wings would spread larger to support that boated body. It did not happen! The butterfly was never able to fly; it only crawled around with its swollen body and shriveled wings.

In his desire to make things easier for the butterfly, the man had perverted the process. The butterfly needed to struggle through that small opening in the cocoon in order to squeeze the fluid from its body into the wings. The struggle would have prepared the butterfly for flight.

A life without hurdles may leave us woefully unprepared for Satan's raging fire. If our faith has faced few challenges, we may find it difficult spread our wings and fly when the sparks are flying. So, when we are confronted with many obstacles, we are being strengthened. In our hearts we can know there is reason for joy!

*Though the fig tree does not bud and
There are no grapes on the vines,*

*Though the olive crop fails and the fields
Produce no food,*

*Though there are no sheep in the pen and
And no cattle in the stalls,*

*Yet I will rejoice in the Lord, I will be
Be joyful in God my Savior.*

Habakkuk 3:17, 18

LEADER'S GUIDE

To the leader:
The following questions are intended to encourage thoughtful discussion of the key elements in each chapter of this timely study. *Surviving the Raging Fire* offers your study group valuable insight into the urgency of living what we profess to believe.

CHAPTER ONE

1. What are the forces that shape our thinking today? Discuss.

2. The "firebreak" between Christians and the world is not necessarily about distance. What creates a firebreak between Christians and the raging fire of immorality and spiritual decline?

3. What specific lessons can we learn from the Israelites of the Old Testament?

4. What are the visible warning signs that Christians may be in the process of being assimilated back into the world?

5. What can Christians do to effectively influence the world for Jesus Christ?

CHAPTER TWO

1. The words of Jesus in Luke 18:30 seem to teach that we will benefit, even in this life, from living sacrificially for the Lord. How so?

2. What does man hope to accomplish when he accepts sin and lives his own will?

3. Convictions may be sapped or eroded by the presence of sin around us. What can we do to limit our constant exposure to the influence of Satan?

4. List some of the reasons that we sometimes fail to flee sin.

5. In 1 Timothy 6:11, Paul urged Timothy to do more than just "flee sin." How does Matthew 12:43-45 apply to Paul's message?

CHAPTER THREE

1. In what ways can a spirit of fearfulness hinder our Christian walk?

2. In what ways do our emotions effect our judgment? Are our emotions reliable?

3. How does doing the right thing and taking responsibility for finding right answers give us stability in times of trial?

4. Discuss how adversity might make us stronger? Does Scripture teach this?

5. Discuss 1 Peter 1:6, 7. Does it explain why grief is sometimes allowed?

CHAPTER FOUR

1. What is there about learning to be grateful that causes us to be happier?

2. Why does focus upon "self" make us miserable?

3. What are some of the ways that selfishness affects relationships in families?

4. In what way is selfishness the opposite of love?

5. List some of the specific sins that have their root in selfishness.

CHAPTER FIVE

1. How many factors can you list which might contribute to a child's going astray?

2. Proverbs 19:13 points out, "A foolish son is his father's ruin." How fine is the line between the concern for reputation and genuine concern for the soul of the child?

3. Adam, Jacob, Eli, Samuel, and David each had sons who went astray. What was the Lord's single criticism of their parenting?

4. Is the subject of discipline and restraint controversial today? What does Scripture teach about discipline?

5. Should a parent try to maintain a relationship with a wayward son or daughter?

CHAPTER SIX

1. Why does God not spare believers the adversities of this life? Do think that we could understand if He explained?

2. Do times of prosperity and success draw us closer in our walk with God?

3. What are the primary emotions involved when we feel anger toward God? Discuss.

4. How can we grow a faith that will endure a culture of immorality and spiritual decline?

5. What is left when we turn away from God?

CHAPTER SEVEN

1. Is a Christian charged with the responsibility to rebuke and condemn sin? In what circumstances?

2. What do you think that a parent should do if a son or daughter announces that he or she is homosexual?

3. If the woman taken in adultery (John 8) had decided to continue her adulterous life, would she have been welcomed as one of Jesus' followers?

4. What kind of person is most likely to restore a sinner?

5. Is it right to ignore ongoing sin in someone with whom we have a close relationship?

CHAPTER EIGHT

1. What kind of resume does one need in order to be used by God?

2. List some of our goals in life. Do they match favorably with God's purpose for us?

3. God's purpose is used as a singular noun in Scripture What is that singular purpose?

4. Why do we fail to recognize our gifts and opportunities?

5. In what circumstances does God do some of His best work in us?